# LONG YEARS *of* EXILE

## Central Asian Refugees in Afghanistan and Pakistan

Dr. Audrey C. Shalinsky

Department of Anthropology
University of Wyoming

UNIVERSITY
PRESS OF
AMERICA

Lanham • New York • London

Portions of Chapters 1, 4, and 6 are reprinted from a work by the
same author in *Die Ethnischen Gruppen Afghanistan,* (Erwin
Orywal, ed.), 1986 by permission of Dr. Ludwig Reichert Verlag.

Portions of Chapters 2 and 3 are reprinted from a work by the same
author in the *Journal of South Asian and Middle Eastern Studies* 3
(2), 1979, by permission.

Portions of Chapter 5 are reprinted from a work by the same author
in *Ethos* 14 (4), December 1986, by permission of the American
Anthropological Association.

Portions of Chapters 5, 8, and 9 are reprinted from a forthcoming
work by the same author in the *International Journal of Middle
East Studies,* by permission of Cambridge University Press.

**Library of Congress Cataloging-in-Publication Data**

Shalinsky, Audrey.
Long years of exile : Central Asian refugees in Afghanistan and
Pakistan / Audrey C. Shalinsky.
p.    cm.
Includes bibliographical references.
1. Uzbeks—Afghanistan—History.   2. Tajiks—Afghanistan—
History.   3. Refugees—Afghanistan.   4. Refugees—Pakistan.
I. Title.
DS354.6.U82S5     1993
954.91'004943—dc20     93–27034 CIP

ISBN 0–8191–9286–4 (cloth : alk. paper)

 The paper used in this publication meets the minimum requirements of
American National Standard for Information Sciences—Permanence
of Paper for Printed Library Materials, ANSI Z39.48–1984.

To My Parents

# Acknowledgements

Since I have worked on some of the materials in this book since 1976, it would be impossible for me to thank everyone who has helped me since then. Still I want to acknowledge those who have encouraged me to continue this research.

At Harvard Nur Yalman first advised me to go to northern Afghanistan and has consistently urged me to publish this account. Michael Fischer provided important advice for my dissertation which continues to inspire me. Thomas Barfield, a colleague from graduate school days, Bahram Tavakolian, whom I first met in Afghanistan, along with Louis and Nancy Dupree, were all important influences on my fieldwork. Eden Naby's publications always make the connections between Central Asian and Afghanistan more clear. The scholarly contributions of Robert Canfield and Nazif Shahrani to Afghan studies have been crucial to the development of my ideas especially to the analysis in Part III.

In Afghanistan in 1975 and 1976-1977, the Afghan-American Educational Commission, under Larry Beck and John Summers and their staff, helped me obtain the necessary permissions from the Cultural Section of the Ministry of Foreign Affairs. The hospitality of the British Institute for Afghan Studies and the Heidelberg South Asia Institute was also appreciated. I also acknowledge the assistance of Abdul Matin of the Afghanistan desk at the Pakistan Ministry of Foreign Affairs for the research I conducted there in 1990.

Since 1980 I have prospered in the Anthropology department at the University of Wyoming. I thank the current chair Anne Slater who has read this manuscript in its entirety. In addition Dean of the College of Arts and Sciences Oliver Walter and Provost Al Karnig facilitated my 1990 sabbatical. Nelda Hernandez typed some portions of this manuscript on the computer and Kathleen Fowler also provided secretarial support. Marian Collins did an excellent job reworking maps and illustrations.

There is no question that those people with whom I worked in Afghanistan and Pakistan, especially those who allowed me to live in their households, made this publication possible. I also thank those individuals in the Uzbek section of Voice of America who have helped me over the years. The final form of the analyses and interpretations offered here is my own responsibility.

# Table of Contents

# Illustrations

# Note on Transliteration

In this book I transliterate many Persian terms according to the consonantal system used in the *International Journal of Middle Eastern Studies*. Vowel sounds are somewhat problematic. For the vowel sound in "how," I use "aw," thus *qawm*, as the word for ethnic group rather than *qaum* as it is sometimes written. For both Persian and Uzbek, the main aim was to enable the reader to approximate the pronunciation. To facilitate reader recognition, some terms, especially place names for which there is historical English usage, are anglicized, for example, Ferghana rather than Farghana. Plurals of foreign words have been formed by adding "s" though occasionally Arabic plurals are also used, thus for the word, emigrants, generally *muhajirs* and sometimes *muhajirin*. I have omitted diacritical marks for a cleaner appearing text. Parentheses are used for translations while brackets are used for author's additional comments to quoted material.

The following measurements are used consistently in the text:

*jerib*=approximately 1/2 acre and .2 hectare

*ser*=7 kilograms

afghani (afs)=unit of currency of which 45=$1.00 in 1977.

# Long Years of Exile

## Central Asian Refugees in Afghanistan and Pakistan

### Introduction

*And those that emigrated in God's cause after they were wronged--We shall surely lodge them in this world in a goodly lodging, and the wage of the world to come is greater, did they but know even such men as are patient, and put their trust in their Lord.* (Quran XVI:41-42 in Arberry 1976:290).

This story begins in the fertile valleys and towns of Central Asia, the area known to medieval Arab geographers as Mawerannahr, literally, the trans-river region. The Ancient Greeks called the rivers Oxus and Jaxartes; and the Persians called them the Amu and Syr Darya. Today the area is the Ferghana Valley, part of Uzbekistan, a former constituent republic of the Soviet Union. The people of this region are predominantly Uzbeks, whose native language is related to Turkish, and Tajiks, who speak a dialect of Persian, an Indo-European language.

In the 1920s and 1930s during the Stalinist era in the Soviet Union, groups of people from the Ferghana Valley joined others who were clandestinely moving across the border into northern Afghanistan with the hope that they could maintain Islam and their cultural traditions in the face of forced and rapid social change. Afghanistan had provided them a refuge for less than half a century when a Marxist government, which took power in 1978, spontaneous uprisings, and subsequent Soviet invasion led many to leave their new homeland for Pakistan, Saudi Arabia, Turkey and other parts of the world. Just as some of their ancestors had fought the Russians, then the Soviets, a guerilla force composed of the sons and grandsons of the emigrants joined the Afghan *mujahidin* and continued the struggle in northern Afghanistan against the Marxist government until its fall.

In 1976 as a PhD candidate in social anthropology at Harvard University working on my doctoral dissertation, I began to study the Ferghana people in Kunduz, a provincial capital in northern Afghanistan and I have continued research into their history and culture since that time. Most recently during the winter of 1990, I completed a visit to Karachi, Pakistan, where many reside as non-registered refugees in several urban neighborhoods, and I was able to meet with individuals whom I had known over fifteen years ago.

I went to northern Afghanistan upon the advice of Professor Nur Yalman, Harvard anthropologist, who knew that as an undergraduate at the University of Chicago I had studied Russian language and history. Professor Yalman believed that research on Uzbeks in Afghanistan would shed light on "sovietized" Uzbeks in the USSR. He and I were intrigued by the ideas of the late Professor Alexandre

1

Bennigsen, an expert on Soviet Muslims, who had written that the various nationalities of the USSR would create problems which would lead to the ultimate demise of that state, an interesting prophecy in light of the ethnic violence that has plagued the now disintegrated empire.

Still when I went to Afghanistan, I intended to study village Uzbeks. It was not in my mind to search out those people who had left Soviet Central Asia for Afghanistan since I did not know that such people existed. However, as they might say, it was *qismat*, luck or fate, which led me to the dispersed community of the people who had come from the Ferghana Valley. I had difficulties setting up my research in a field location and sought the advice of John Summers, then director of the Afghan-American Educational Commission, the agency which helped researchers obtain governmental permissions. As I listed possible field locations in northern Afghanistan, I was interrupted when I mentioned Kunduz. The director knew a high school teacher from the town of Kunduz who was an Uzbek.

I met the teacher at the director's home in Kabul, the capital of Afghanistan. We began to talk about the possibility of fieldwork in Kunduz. When I asked about his ethnic background, I was surprised to learn that his parents had come from the Ferghana Valley in Uzbekistan. In fact, many of the people in his neighborhood had come from the same small town in the Ferghana Valley, the town of Kasan. Others in Kunduz were from areas in or near Namangan, Andijan, Kokand, and Tashkent, the major cities of the Ferghana Valley. Soon I travelled to Kunduz to meet his family to see if they would agree for me to live with them for the period of my study. Though I had travelled in northern Afghanistan during the summer of 1975 on an earlier visit, I had not seen Kunduz. Before new Kunduz was built in the 1930s, the old town had had the reputation of a deathtrap. A common saying was, "Go to Kunduz and die," referring to endemic malaria from the swampy mosquito-infested land in the environs of the town (Byron 1937:260-261). The new Kunduz was a prosperous city, an agro-industrial center of cotton production.

> Kunduz might be termed a kind of Afghan California, where people have drifted in from all parts of the country for jobs and new land, and have developed a generalized dialect and way of life, while keeping roots in the old homeland and maintaining some local traditions (Slobin 1976: 157).

Kunduz was a major center for the emigrants from Soviet Central Asia including Uzbeks, Tajiks, and Kazakhs who were generally referred to as *muhajirin*, an Arabic word used in the Quran, Islam's holy book, as the term for the righteous followers of the Prophet Muhammad who were persecuted by the

Meccans and fled to Medina where they formed part of the *umma,* the fledgling Muslim community and nascent state.

*Muhajirin* [or *muhajirs*] is usually translated as "emigrants" in English versions of the Quran. However, the word carries much in its Islamic context along with the core denotation of migration. It implies people who are obligated to make *hijrat,* to leave their homes for God's sake. When an illegitimate non-Islamic government comes to control a region which should be controlled by an Islamic government, good Muslims must conduct *jihad,* struggle to restore legitimate government and, if necessary, they must leave their homes, make *hijrat,* become *muhajirin* rather than submit to improper rule. Those who left Central Asia rather than submit to the Soviet transformation of their society therefore took the title of *muhajirin.* Additionally, since the war against the Marxist government of Afghanistan was *jihad,* a struggle against an illegitimate non-Islamic government, all the Afghans in Pakistan and Iran are also *muhajirin.*

In publications on the Afghanistan War, *muhajir,* is frequently translated as "refugee," but this usage omits the entire Islamic sense of the term. *Jihad* and *Hijrat* are conceptually linked. When *jihad* is conducted, men move their families to a place of refuge first; they do *hijrat.* Similarly, making *hijrat* implies that there is an on-going *jihad* against a government perceived as essentially flawed. The Ferghana people then are twice *muhajirin,* a fact of particular significance today.

It has only been within the last few years that anthropologists have located groups who are "culturally displaced" at the center of analysis. Refugees, people without territorial homelands or nation-states, immigrant individuals who are known to have moved across borders are a new focus for analysis (Rosaldo 1989, Malkki 1992). One important purpose of these studies is to illustrate the complex means by which people construct, remember, and claim connection to specific places to which they are not physically joined. Some researchers see cultural displacement as a key post-modern metaphor because a generalized condition of homelessness for everyone characterizes the contemporary world (Said 1979). This study then illuminates a particular historical and ethnographic case of displaced or "transnational persons" spanning most of the twentieth century. It shows their ever expanding "homeland," first as they move across a single "national" border marked by a river, then more moves covering greater and greater distances to neighboring countries, then within the Middle East-South Asia region, and finally across oceans around the world.

A refugee or immigrant group, or for that matter, any group, which finds itself in a situation of rapid social change, must rediscover how to maintain or maximize economic resources, how to improve political positions, and how to compete in new institutional frameworks (Eisenstadt 1974:20). An even greater problem for an immigrant group is the attempt to retain and simultaneously reformulate identity. This study will describe the variety of ways the Ferghanachis have attempted to sort out the problem of identity. From the Afghanistan of the 1930s to the United States of the 1990s, they have struggled and sought to forge a meaningful set of reconstructions of the past, perceptions of the present and plans for the future. Because they have dealt with widely different social environments, technologies and societies, they provide a lesson in both steadfastness and flexibility.

A related theme of this study involves the ways individuals, searching within and without, reorganize, emotionally and intellectually, old and new cultural symbols so that congruent personal identities are created. Life histories and stories focussed on individuals linked either by kinship or neighborhood association and historical origins are provided. The Ferghanachis' sense of themselves as Muslims has been a core component of their continued survival as a community. In successive countries of refuge, they have retained a value system permeated with the daily routine of Islamic observance. In this, those who have come to the United States may face their greatest challenge.

The book is divided into three major sections. Part I explains who the Ferghanachis are historically. Their ethnicity and language affiliation are examined in the Central Asian context. The conquest of Central Asia by the Russians and the subsequent turmoil of the early Soviet period result in the loss of the homeland as the Ferghanachis emigrate to Afghanistan and reconstruct their community in exile for the first time. The role of Islamic identity and values are intrinsic to the emigration. Part II places the Ferghanachis as their community existed in northern Afghanistan just before the Marxist coup. Islamic values are shown to be basic to the lifestyle in such areas as family life, gender relations, neighborhood ties, ethnicity, religiosity and even material culture. The stage is set for the second and still continuing emigration and transformation of the community. Part III records the situation in Afghanistan during the last ten plus years and the movement of the community into Pakistan and beyond. The participation of the Ferghanachis in the on-going Afghanistan *jihad*, their politics and their role in the Islamic resurgence today are explained. The Ferghanachis confront the future in the United States, Pakistan and Afghanistan and with Uzbekistan, the original homeland, also in transition. Their abilities to cope with these varying changes again revolve around the reformulation of Islam. This book takes Part III 1990 and the second exile as the ethnographic present, and therefore Part II, the 1970s, as the ethnographic past.

# Part I

The Central Asian Context

# Chapter 1

# Language, Ethnicity, Geography

Central Asia is described in historical documents from many parts of the world. In his sixteenth century memoirs, Tamerlane's grandson Babur, the founder of the Moghul dynasty of India whose homeland was Mawerannahr, writes of the beauty of his ancestral territory between the rivers, Syr and Amu. Babur knew the lands immediately south of the Amu Darya as Balkh and farther east as Badakhshan while northern Iran and the western Afghan plateau he called Khorasan. Because of invading armies which defeated his forces, Babur was forced to flee from the homeland that he loved first south of Balkh to Afghanistan and then farther to the east. In many ways the *muhajirs* of the twentieth century have recapitulated Babur's journey from Mawerannahr to Afghanistan to Pakistan.

Babur's homeland Mawerannahr, known in European historical sources as Transoxiana or Transoxania, the land beyond the Oxus, has also been referred to as Turkestan, land of the Turks, because of its Turkic-speaking population groups. The upper valley of the Syr Darya was called Davan by Chinese sources and apparently, Parkan was the corresponding term used by the ancient Greeks. The word, "Ferghana," is derived from Parkan (Oshanin 1964, II:36). The Ferghana Valley, Babur's own starting point is also the beginning of the journey for the *muhajirs*. Map 1.1 indicates the region between the Syr and Amu in Central Asia.

In order to understand the *muhajirs'* migration, several crucial sources of group identity: language, religion, ethnicity, and geography, must be set within the appropriate Central Asian contexts. The original population of ancient Turkestan was of the same Iranian stock as the Persians. During the sixth century, the first wave of Turkic speakers entered the region. Though the Turks and Persians intermingled, Persian influence remained strong, especially in urban areas. Many city dwellers during this time may have been Zoroasterians (Caroe 1967:49). The Arab Muslim conquest of the 7th-8th centuries did not diminish the dominance of Persian culture. Fifty years after the conquest, civil disorder fostered by the Ummayyad inegalitarian policies toward the rights of non-Arab Muslims led to violence. The Abbassids of Baghdad, the new Islamic ruling dynasty, gave power in Turkestan to the Khorasanis of eastern Iran. Persian influence therefore also came to be associated with Islam. The Karakhanid and Seljuk invasions of the

7

area during the eleventh century, which included new Turkic groups from the east, increased Turkicization[1] of language but even the Mongol invasion did not result in large scale disruptive social change. New groups who remained in Central Asia assimilated into the pre-existing local population, adopting Turkic languages, Islam, and Persianized culture.

According to some historians, the traditional distinction of Central Asian peoples was not ethnic or linguistic, but was based upon subsistence pattern, nomadic pastoralism or sedentary agriculturism (Bennigsen 1967:24). The sedentary element considered itself first as Muslim, and after that, as inhabiting a town or a definite district (Barthold 1934:175-176). Supposedly, indigenous norm and practice was that sedentary communities, regardless of origin and language, considered themselves as distinct from the Turkic-speaking nomads. The nomads called the sedentary people, Sarts, a Turkic word derogatorily denoting trader or merchant or sometimes, Tajiks, even when they spoke Turkic languages. The nomadic tribes who had entered the area at the time that Shaibani Khan invaded and defeated Babur referred to themselves as Uzbeks.

Russian ethnographers of the Tsarist period following indigenous practice, distinguished between Sart, those of the oasis culture, mostly Turkic but with some Persian speakers; and those who retained some part of tribal and nomadic lifestyle, the Uzbeks. The Soviets regarded this as a false and perjorative practice and they extended the term, "Uzbek" to include all groups speaking related Turkic dialects (Bacon 1966:18).

Many scholars believe that the name Uzbek was eponymously derived from Uzbek, one of the khans of the Golden Horde. Since Uzbek Khan (1312-1340) became Muslim, his name was applied to the Muslim element of the Golden Horde which constituted its ruling class. During the fifteenth century the Uzbeks occupied the country between the Lower Volga and the Aral Sea. They then migrated into Transoxania. Another explanation of the derivation of the term Uzbek, probably a folk etymology, divides it into *oz*, self and *beg*, master. Thus the name has been interpreted as those who are their own masters or "the free people." (Caroe 1967:41).

Tajiks as Persian speakers presumably constitute the oldest ethnic element in Turkestan, but apart from the Persian language and the fact that they are not viewed as having tribal origins, there seems little to distinguish them from the Uzbeks (Naby 1984: 5). The word Tajik may be derived from Tay, the name of an Arab tribe. In the tenth century, Tazi, was used in Transoxania as a general term for all Muslims.

There are current folk stereotypes about the personality structure and character of Tajiks and Uzbeks. Schuyler (1877) related one version of the famous love story of Shirin and Ferhat on this subject.

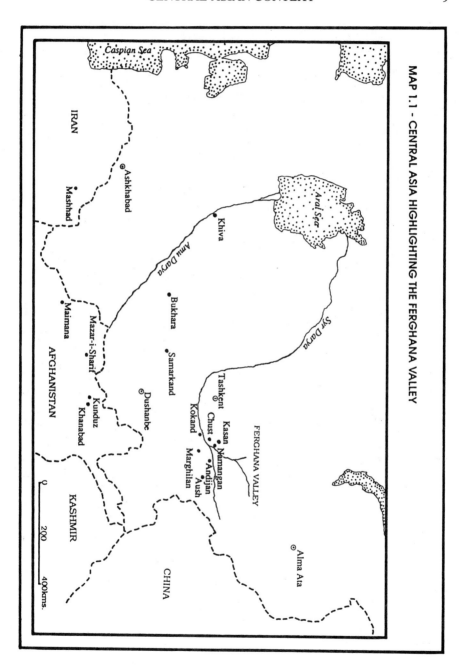

MAP 1.1 - CENTRAL ASIA HIGHLIGHTING THE FERGHANA VALLEY

There was once a queen, Shirin Hatun, of great beauty, who lived on the farther side of the Syr Darya. She had two wooers, one a Tajik and the other an Uzbek named Ferhat. Both were persistent and as she was at a loss which to choose, an old woman counselled her to give them some difficult work and to marry the one who succeeded. She therefore commanded them to dig a canal through the Famished Steppe. Ferhat, a strong stalwart fellow with a simple straightforward nature, took his spade and dug away all day, trying to turn the channel of the river . . . The Tajik, crafty and full of expedients, plaited a wicker of reed and laid it on the ground across the steppe. Early in the morning the sun's rays reflected from the shining reeds made them appear like a stream of water, and Shirin Hatun thereupon called for the Tajik and married him. When the Uzbek learned of the deception that had been practiced upon him, he was in despair and threw his spade up in the air so that as it came down it cut off his head with a single stroke (I:108-109).

So the simple straightforward honest Uzbek was defeated through the craftiness of the tricky Tajik. The stereotype depicted in the story is related to ideas about the simplicity of nomads and farmers versus the shrewdness of urban merchants.

Little is known about Uzbek tribal history. Although the names of the tribes on both sides of the Amu are unsystematically reported,[2] the following are known to exist on both sides of the Amu: Mangyt, Ming, Karluk, Qungrat, Kenegez, Kitay, Kipchak, Kangly, Chagatay, Kattagan, Durmen, Lakai (Jarring 1939). Complicating the situation, however, is the fact that during the unrest in the late part of the Russian and the early part of the Soviet period, groups left the north side of the border, the Amu Darya, and fled to the Afghan side where they either established new villages or joined old ones.[3] These people may have had tribal names which coincided with Uzbeks already settled on the south side of the Amu for hundreds of years. These people perceived themselves and were perceived by other Uzbeks as not from Afghanistan. They were often identified as people "from the other side," referring to the other side of the Amu. During the course of field work, I heard one villager give his tribal name and then say he had come as a small boy from the other side of the river (the Amu); he entered Afghanistan in the period 1910-1915. Others listed some Qungrat, Lakai and Durmen Uzbeks as entering Afghanistan since the Soviet regime.

The Uzbeks with tribal names, whether Afghan or Transoxanian, and the people who provide the subject of this study form two distinct groups. The *muhajirs* from Ferghana gave no tribal names as their own; rather, they offered town names and formed urban neighborhoods in Afghanistan on the basis of common town origin. They could be said to have Sart origins if one were to adhere to pre-Soviet ethnographic terminology. Slobin (1976:104) remarks on the "cultural tenacity" of these people given that they are surrounded by fellow Uzbeks and have not assimilated. This is explicable because two distinctions reinforce each other, one distinction between native and emigrant and the other old one between Sart and Uzbek.

The Ferghana Valley, the original *watan*, homeland, of the *muhajirs* is known as one of the most fertile regions of Central Asia because of the conjunction of the Kara Darya and the Naryn which form the Syr Darya river system. *(See Map 1.1)*

> . . . owing to the fertility of the soil and the excellence of the climate, the agriculture of the khanate [the nineteenth century Kokand khanate] is in a most flourishing condition. Wheat, millet and barley are largely cultivated, the last of poor quality and used only for the food of horses. Rice grows in great abundance everywhere as also lucerne, but the two chief products of the khanate are cotton and silk, which are also the main articles of export . . . The population of the khanate is probably less than a million and is sharply divided into two classes, the settled and the nomad. The settled class inhabits only the open valley, and with the exception of Namangan, and a few towns to the north of the Syr Darya, occupies but a narrow zone between that river and the foot hills, in which most of the towns are situated. The settled population are chiefly Uzbeks: but in Kokand and the region of the west there are a considerable number of Tajiks (Schuyler 1877, II:56).

When my oldest informants, those who had actually come from the Ferghana Valley talked about it, they repeatedly emphasized the superiority of its agricultural produce and general fertility of the land to that of Afghanistan. "In Ferghana, the melons were sweeter and the taste of the food was better than here," said one. While nostalgia for the past cannot be discounted, the emphasis on the superiority of the land and its products was striking.

Map 1.1 indicates the location of the main cities and towns of the Ferghana Valley. Kasan, a town north of the Syr Darya on a tributary called Kasansai, was the home of many informants. Historical evidence indicates that the ethnic composition of Kasan was primarily Tajik. Gault's 1892 ethnographic survey in *L'Anthropologie* concludes that most of the towns to the north of the Syr Darya and west of the Naryn are Tajik with the exception of Namangan while the rest of Ferghana is Uzbek. The pattern has continued through the twentieth century, a more recent Soviet book on Ferghana noting that though Tajiks are in the minority in the Valley, they predominate in the Pansk, Chust and Kasansai districts (Akramov 1960:21).

Kasan was founded in the second century AD at the border between agricultural and grazing land. In the time of the Kushan empire (first to fourth centuries AD), it was the political and economic center of the Ferghana Valley but it fell into decline around the 8th Century AD. In his memoirs, Babur wrote, "Kasan has excellent air and beautiful little gardens. As these gardens all lie along the bed of the torrent, people call them the 'fine front of the coat.'[4] Between Kasanis and Aushis there is rivalry about the beauty and climate of their townships" (Beveridge 1912:10).

The most complete ethnographic account of Kasan was published in 1928 by Mikhail Andreev in the Russian journal, *The Society for Studies of Tajikistan and Iranian Peoples Beyond its Boundaries*. At that time, Kasan was a town of about 3000 households. Andreev states that the majority of the population was Tajik-speaking, but some women spoke Uzbek. He also commented on the many Turkic words which seemed to have replaced older Persian terminology (1928:111). Many of the older residents of the Kasani neighborhood in Kunduz were still in Kasan at the time of Andreev's research. They too knew the Kasani dialect of Tajik and they spoke it only among themselves. Among old men this was especially common. They described their language dialect much as Andreev did as containing a large number of Uzbek words that were then Tajikized, for example, by adding the Persian verb *kardan,* to make or do, to an Uzbek noun, a verbal form was created.

None of the Kasanis ever referred to him or herself as Tajik. Most of them, particularly women, were as fluent in Uzbek as they were in Persian.[5] They explained their bilingualism as having resulted from the fact that in much of the Ferghana Valley including the nearby city of Namangan, Uzbek was the language commonly used. In visiting the bazaar and friends in Namangan, it was convenient to know both languages. The oldest Kasanis who had come from Ferghana also did not refer to themselves as Uzbeks, however, younger men, those born in Afghanistan, did often use this as an identity label.

The *muhajirs* from Kasan made up only a small part of the *muhajir* community in Afghanistan. There were *muhajirs* from all the towns in the Ferghana Valley including Namangan, Andijan, Kokand and Tashkent. Therefore the majority were primarily Uzbek speakers. These people, whether Uzbek or Tajik speaking, viewed themselves as constituting a distinct endogamous group in Afghanistan. Based on informants' estimates, in the 1970s there were perhaps five hundred to one thousand households of Ferghana Valley emigrants in Afghanistan probably between 5,000-10,000 people.

While they preferred to use the Islamic label, *muhajir,* to refer to their group, outsiders called them Ferghanachis or Bukharais. While these seem simple geographic derivations, they were viewed as somewhat derogatory by the *muhajirs,* who felt they emphasized a non-native and inferior status. In Afghanistan the name Ferghanachi was used in some interethnic situations and in the past fifteen years it has become increasingly common.

The labels Ferghanachi and Bukharai incorporated slightly different referents. While Ferghanachi referred to Ferghana Valley emigrants and therefore Uzbek speakers, Bukharai referred to those from the former emirate of Bukhara who tended to be Persian speakers. Northern Afghanistan was full of people of Bukharan origin, many more than there were Feghanachis.

There were differing patterns of linguistic assimilation in Bukhara and Ferghana. Soviet ethnographic research has listed cases in Bukhara in which Tajik speakers still call themselves Uzbeks, maintain kin ties and intermarry with neighboring Uzbek speaking villages. In the Soviet view, these former Uzbeks have become Tajikized. In Ferghana, on the other hand, Tajiks more often become Uzbekized. The population of the city of Marghilan, for example, dropped Tajik and adopted the Uzbek language (Slobin 1976:71-72, 75).

Those outside the *muhajir* community may have used the labels Ferghanachi and Bukharai interchangeably. In fact, Bukharai is the more inclusive term. An informant said that all *muhajirs* use Bukharai when making the pilgrimage to Mecca. They use the ancient Bukharan reputation for Muslim piety and learning to enhance their status. Some of the *muhajirs* who make the *haj* have remained in Saudi Arabia where they have a flourishing community much increased in population after the Marxist government in Afghanistan came to power in 1978.

## NOTES

1. The Karakhanids were the first Turkish ruling house to embrace Islam. The convert was Bughra Khan of Kashgar, Eastern Turkestan whose grandson conquered Bukhara and Samarkand in 999. A folktale version of this conversion is found in Jarring 1938:142-155.

2. The exact number of Uzbeks in Afghanistan has been reported as 1-1.5 million for over 25 years. Uzbeks themselves state that there are as many as 3 millon Uzbeks in Afghanistan. Obviously, the Afghan government was reluctant to indicate precisely how many non-Pashtuns were in the country. Soviet sources fail to discuss those Uzbeks who left the Soviet Union for Afghanistan. One source on the Uzbeks in Afghanistan is Naby 1984.

3. Robert Byron, an explorer who travelled the region on the Afghan side of the border in the 1930s, reported that "huge bands of Turcomans have crossed the river from Russia and settled themselves in the jungle on the south bank" (1937:252).

4. This saying metaphorically refers to the embroidered edge of a *chapan,* the cotton/silk cloak worn by Central Asian men.

5. Because women have fewer contacts with outsiders, they retain Uzbek with less interference from other languages (Nazif Shahrani, personal communication, 1985).

# Chapter 2

## The Arrival of the Russians in Turkestan

A leader of Turko-Persian heritage, Timur, known as Tamerlane in the West, gained power in Mawerrannahr in 1369. Under Timur and his successors, literature and the arts flourished. Timur and his descendants considered themselves Turks; they wrote in the Turkic language, Chagatay, and also in Persian. Babur, a descendant of Timur, lost his Central Asian empire to yet another Turkic-speaking group, the Uzbeks under the leadership of Shaibani Khan. Shaibani Khan's success against Babur encouraged him to move south of the Amu Darya where he seized the city-states of Kunduz, Badakhshan, Balkh and Herat. He then challenged Ismail, founder of the Safavid dynasty of Persia, and was defeated and killed at the battle of Merv in 1510, resulting in the loss of Khorasan and the lands south of the Amu Darya, the pattern of the present frontier between the former Soviet Union, Afghanistan, and Iran (Map 2.1). From this time on, power south of the Amu was held by small Uzbek city-states for whom there were times of autonomy, times of dependence on Bukhara or Delhi (India), and times of defeat by Persian and Afghan (N. Dupree 1967).

At the end of the eighteenth century, two new Uzbek dynasties were founded, the Mangyt in Bukhara and the Qungrat in Khorezm, the latter then becoming known as Khiva. After a mid-nineteenth century revolt against Bukhara, a third khanate was formed in Kokand by powerful nobles of Ferghana, who were of the Uzbek tribal group Ming and had ruled there intermittently since the beginning of the eighteenth century.

South of the Amu, the Pashtun monarchs of Afghanistan gradually encroached upon the Uzbek lands north of the Hindu Kush Mountains. Ahmad Shah Durrani, known as the father of modern Afghanistan, incorporated Balkh into his domain in 1759, but within ten years the people there revolted at the instigation of the Amir of Bukhara. Ahmad Shah regained control over Balkh, but after his death, Uzbek leaders of Kunduz, Tashkurghan and Samangan vied for power in the region. By 1859, Amir Dost Muhammad of Kabul had more firmly established Afghan control, and Balkh became the capital of Afghan Turkestan. The stability of the political situation in Transoxania and Afghan Turkestan was not again seriously interrupted until the arrival of the Russians north of the Amu in the last decades of the nineteenth century. Amir Abd al-Rahman Khan, king of Afghanistan from 1880-1901, did implement a policy of resettling political dissidents, mostly from rival Pashtun tribes, to areas, including northern Afghanistan, far from their homes. He confiscated their traditional land holdings and added them to the

15

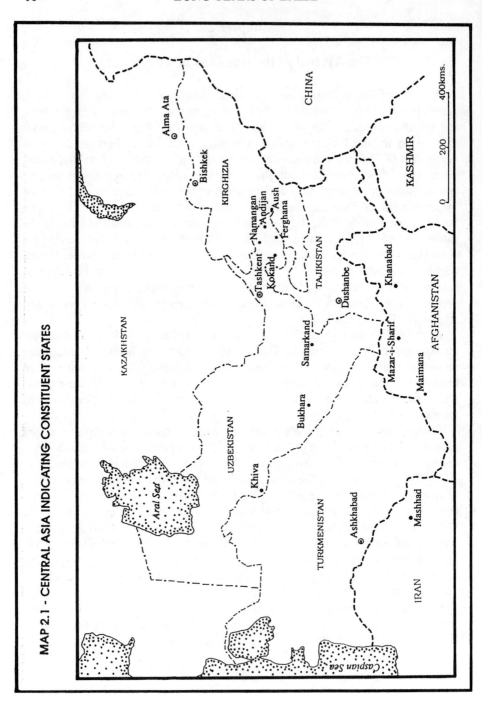

MAP 2.1 - CENTRAL ASIA INDICATING CONSTITUENT STATES

government revenue. He also encouraged voluntary migration by nomadic Pashtuns to the north by granting tax concessions, road expenses and provisions for grain and agricultural equipment for the purposes of national security (N. Tapper 1983: 233-261; L. Dupree 1989:34).[1]

The khanates of Bukhara, Khiva, and Kokand confronted significant Russian expansionism during the last part of the nineteenth century. In 1855, a Russian army column moved into Turkestan, capturing several towns. In 1868, they conquered Samarkand and the Amir of Bukhara was obliged to sign a treaty by which his state was placed under Russian protection. The khanate of Khiva became a protectorate in 1873; Kokand surrendered in 1876 and that khanate, which included the Ferghana Valley, was abolished. That area was placed under direct Russian control through a military administration constituted as a governate-general and was renamed Russian Turkestan. The colonized Muslims were not subject to military service and preserved their own juridical status in conformance with Muslim law.

In Russian Turkestan beginning in 1885, the indigenous population expressed its hostility toward the Russian conquerors through sporadic revolts. These revolts generally followed a pattern of *jihad*, often with the idea of restoring the Kokand khanate. The revolts were usually led by religious leaders, frequently of the Sufi order, Naqshbandiyya; their troops were farmers and town artisans (Carrere d'Encausse 1967:163, 1988:66). The call to *jihad* was spread through the mosques. Evidence for this comes from the American explorer Schuyler's account of a visit to a sufi meeting in Samarkand. Public sermons had been forbidden by the Russian authorities.

> When I was about to go the chief addressed me a petition saying that this establishment of dervishes had been founded long ago for pious uses; that it was devoted to the reception of the poor, the sick and the blind, and of persons who had no other refuge and that the only means they had to support it was by taking contributions from the faithful throughout the city. They begged me therefore to represent to the authorities the religious and charitable objects they had in view and to request that they might be allowed as before to recite their prayers and to preach their sermons in public . . . I told the prefect afterwards of the request . . . which he was not at all astonished to hear; but he said, that however they might deny it, instances of their treasonable language were only too well proved because officers, frequently in passing by unobserved, had heard parts of their sermons which usually consist of the narration of some old legend where the people were enslaved by the infidel on account of their irreligious life and practices; and end with an appeal to repentances saying that thus the infidel may be driven away (1877, I: 288).

The 1885 revolt in Ferghana was led by a landowner who had apparently served the fallen khan. He roused the districts of Andijan, Aush and Marghilan. Russian troops put down the rebellion, arrested large numbers of people and executed some. The Russian military administration recorded this type of violent confrontation as occurring hundreds of times; sometimes, as in Namangan in 1891, there was nearly full-scale rebellion. In the early 1890s, riots in Tashkent were provoked when the Russian authorities introduced cholera prevention measures which shocked local sensibilities such as sanitary inspections (the local population refused to allow the examination of women) and insistence that the dead be hastily buried in a new and distant cemetery. Rioters even destroyed the headquarters of the Russian commander.

Another serious revolt occurred in 1898 in Andijan. The leader was a Naqshbandi sufi who had supervised the construction of a *madrassah* (school), two mosques and a library. 546 men were tried by the Russians and six were hanged. Certain villages accused of aiding in the rebellion were destroyed and the land given to Russian colonists (Carrere d'Encausse 1967:164-169, 1988:67).

Following the Andijan revolt, Kukhovsky, the new governor-general for Russian Turkestan wrote:

> I am forced to the conclusion that this area is far from peaceful; that the embers of religious and national hatred for their conquerors skillfully concealed by gratitude for the material benefits brought into the area, were ready at the first opportunity to burst into flames . . . Our widespread lack of interest in Islam which is a very stable and certainly hostile force should be considered harmful to Russian interests (as quoted in Wheeler 1964:89)

Despite these numerous episodes of native revolt, Russia's colonial grip tightened. Though few Russian settlers came into Russian Turkestan, economic exploitation was in full operation by 1900. The area under cotton cultivation grew from 13,200 hectares in 1886 to 597,200 hectares in 1914 (Rywkin 1963:29). This boom in cotton production was combined with an increasing grain deficit. Russian Turkestan, previously self-supporting in grain, now had to import grain from other parts of Russia. While Russian Turkestan exported raw cotton, imports of Russian cotton textiles also increased.

The worst effects of monocropping were confined to the Ferghana Valley. Bukhara and Khiva were less affected. In the first decade of the twentieth century, 5 percent of cultivated land in Bukhara was in cotton and 50 percent was in wheat. In the Ferghana oblast, which contained almost two thirds of the total cotton acreage of Russian Turkestan and Transcaspia, 36-38 percent of the total arable land was planted in cotton and in some sub-districts the figure was as high as 95 percent (Becker 1968:183).

During World War I, grain shipments in Russian Turkestan slowed as additional grain was needed at the front. Small-scale famines occurred nearly every year. With the October Revolution and subsequent civil war, grain shipments ceased completely. No cotton could be transported, so prices fell as it piled up in warehouses and the new Soviet government began to fix prices. When this stopped the flow of goods to markets, the government began to requisition grain and other commodities from peasants. Because peasants feared confiscation, they ceased production. Land under cultivation declined to one-half its pre-revolutionary extent. There were estimates that by 1919 one-half the population was starving (Park 1957:38). A demographic study of the Soviet Union indicates that during World War I, the only areas of absolute population decrease were the North Caucasus and Turkestan. The loss in Turkestan of 1.23 million people is "attributed to the rebellion against conscription for military labor in 1916, to disorders involving 'mass executions' and the movement of people across borders into Chinese Turkestan and Afghanistan (Lorimer 1946:30).

## Early Soviet Period

During the period of the Russian Revolution and Civil War, guerilla warfare reached its height in Russian Turkestan. The Russians called their opponents Basmachis which meant bandits or brigands supposedly from the Turkic word, *basmak*, to raid. Various organized peasant bands of brigands had appeared as early as 1905 as the voice of the dispossessed, the landless in Ferghana (Carrere d'Encausee 1988:73). The Basmachis, however, were much more than a bandit organization, they nearly became a national liberation movement.

The movement began in the Ferghana Valley. In February 1918, the newly created Muslim autonomous Kokand government was overthrown by the Red army (Naby 1986b:292). The Tashkent Soviet's policies increased support for the Basmachis. Requisitions for bread and cotton, the shooting of peasants suspected of sympathizing with the Basmachis, and looting by Red troops played in favor of the guerillas. The revolt continued with Soviet military actions against Khiva and Bukhara, the Amir of Bukhara having fled to the eastern part of his territory where he joined various Uzbek leaders and their forces who also became known as Basmachis. The Amir was joined by Enver Pasha (known in Central Asia as Anwar Beg), who had been the leading figure in the Young Turk triumverate. Condemned to death by the government of Kemal Ataturk, Enver went to Germany and then to the Soviet Union with hopes of gaining allies against the British. In March 1921, when the Bolsheviks made a treaty with Ataturk, Enver switched allegiance to the

Basmachis and the movement would perhaps have taken on a Pan-Turkic cast had not Enver been killed in August in a battle with a Russian force.

Meanwhile in the Ferghana Valley, the Basmachis had won control of the countryside and the towns of Marghilan, Namangan and Andijan. Under the leadership of Kurshimat (Kurbashi Shir Muhammad), they destroyed cotton mills and the railway line; they made contact with liberal intellectuals in Bukhara and with Russian anti-Bolshevik groups. The Red army was not successful against them until the summer of 1921, when its troops were reinforced. By 1922 Soviet authorities understood that military measures were most effective when combined with political and economic concessions. The offer of amnesty attracted many peasants who wished to return to their agricultural work. Soviet troops prevented contact between urban and rural areas. Food was imported into the towns but the rural people and the Basmachis suffered famine. In March 1923, Soviet authorities offered the peasants food on condition they keep it for themselves and plant cotton. The Basmachis were forced to extort food and they began to lose rural support. The Soviets also curtailed the attack on Islam and began to placate Muslim clergy and even used outside Muslim troops in the fight against locals (Naby 1986b: 293).

Many of the local leaders and small groups of their followers fled to Afghanistan from which they continued to raid Soviet territory. One famous leader, Ibrahim beg, was not captured until 1931. The lack of support by the various monarchs of Afghanistan with the exception of the short-lived reign of Habibullah II broke the back of the Basmachi movement. There was no place for refuge and regrouping (Naby 1986b:294). Emigre Turkestani newspapers published in Germany reported outbreaks of violence continuing along the Soviet-Afghan border until 1951.

The results of the sustained warfare were devastating. In Tajikistan, two-thirds of the arable land was abandoned while in Uzbekistan, the figure was about one-fourth (Rywkin 1963:60). During the Civil War and famine, peasants had returned to the cultivation of grain crops. Though by 1927, raw cotton production was 98.6 percent of the 1914 total, crop acreage was only 80 percent and gross agricultural output 76 percent of the 1914 level (Central Asian Review 1964:41). The population of the city of Kokand which was 120,000 before the Revolution was only 69,300 in 1926 (Pipes 1964:176).

During the time of the Basmachi revolt, Bolshevik authorities, through the Tashkent Soviet, sought to introduce a number of major economic and social reforms which would have fundamentally altered traditional Central Asian society. Because of the chaotic conditions that prevailed until the late 1920s, collectivization of agriculture, educational and legal reform, and anti-religious agitation were postponed. The period 1928-1938 marked the resurgence of these concerns with increasing pressure toward the transformation of traditional society.

The first collective farms were set up in 1918 on some of the big nationalized estates. By 1929 about 1.8 percent of the reduced area under cultivation was collectivized. In those early years, many peasants joined collective farms only to gain government subsidies and confiscated land. Landlords themselves set up collective farms to prevent confiscation. Nearly all these farms failed. By 1924 in all of Uzbekistan there were only 62 collective farms. The Communist Party found it difficult to persuade poorer peasants that their richer neighbors were class enemies. Collective farms, village soviets and electoral commissions had to constantly be purged of "hostile class elements," merchants, mullahs, and former Basmachis.

During the early 1930s, the Communist Party continued to urge peasants to join collectives, offering tax concessions, free building materials and other incentives. During the years 1930-34, more than forty thousand small holdings constituting over 5 percent of the peasant holdings in Uzbekistan were liquidated. By 1937, the party supposedly had achieved the goal of complete collectivization (Central Asian Review 1964:40-52).

In Turkestan, the educational and legal systems were intimately connected with Islam. Much of community life revolved around the village or neighborhood mosque. The war against Islam followed much the same pattern as the collectivization campaign. Early harsh measures implemented by the Tashkent Soviet were rescinded because of native reaction, but the measures were eventually reintroduced. For example, at the time of the Revolution, a major source of income for mosques, *waqf* lands, land trusts from which profits supported the religious institution, accounted for between 8 and 10 percent of cultivated lands in Central Asia. The Tashkent Soviet expropriated the *waqf* lands, but they were restored in 1922. Beginning in 1925, these lands were again taken over with an advertising campaign that the confiscated land would be distributed to peasants. There was then little resistance to the confiscation (Bennigsen 1967:145).

In 1916, in the Ferghana Valley alone, there were 7,290 *maktabs* (primary schools) with 70,000 students, and 375 *madrassahs* (secondary schools) with 9,600 students. The disappearance of *waqf* lands providing financial support and the establishment of Soviet schools led to the end of these Islamic schools. By 1927, there were only 250 *maktabs* left and the next year even these were officially closed (Bennigsen 1967:148). Religious instruction could only be obtained secretly. In fact, beginning in 1928, no formal education was given in the Arabic alphabet. A latinized form for the Turkic languages and Tajik was used from 1928 until 1940 when the Cyrillic alphabet was adopted.

In 1917, the Tashkent Soviet resolved to close the *Shariat* (religious law) and *adat* (customary law) courts, but could not enforce the measure. They tolerated a dual system whereby these courts could not pronounce decisions in conflict with Soviet law. In 1923 the authority of the *shariat* court was weakened by providing for the transfer of civil cases if one of the parties objected to the religious court. In 1924 any criminal or civil action was transferred to the Soviet court if the monetary sum involved was over 25 rubles. Brideprice payment, polygyny or simultaneous marriage to more than one woman, and leviratic marriage were made punishable by imprisonment. The number of religious courts decreased. From 1922-24, the number of *shariat* courts in Ferghana, Zerafshan, Samarkand and Syr Darya declined from 342 to 99. The courts were stripped of all legal status and by 1927, only 17 remained.

Beginning in 1928, mullahs and mosque leaders were persecuted not just as parasites but as counter-revolutionaries and after 1935 as Japanese and German spies. The pilgrimage to Mecca and the payment of *zakat*, alms, two of the five religious duties or pillars of Islam, were prohibited. Fasting during the month of Ramadan, another of the five pillars, was attacked. Finally, the campaign came for the closure of the mosques themselves. The number of mosques in the Turkestan Governate-General, Bukhara, Khiva and the steppe region was estimated as twenty thousand in 1917. In 1953, the Mufti of Tashkent gave the probably high estimate of 200 mosques serving the same region and a greatly increased population. Western researchers believe unofficial clergy and mosques continued to operate (Wheeler 1964:191).

## NOTES

1. These Pashtun remigrated to south and southwestern Afghanistan after the 1979 Soviet invasion (L. Dupree 1989:35).

# Chapter 3

## Migration to Afghanistan

From the preceding narrative of the events in Turkestan from 1917-1939, a two-stage process of sovietization in apparent. Stage 1, from 1917-28, is a continuation of Russian colonial rule and indigenous reaction. "The brazenly colonialist demeanor of the Tashkent Soviet had provoked a popular uprising--the Basmachi movement which was properly speaking anti-Russian and not anti-Bolshevik" (Bennigsen 1967:94). Although there was economic chaos because of the guerilla warfare, society as a whole had not been disrupted. In fact, because of the lack of Muslim Marxists in 1920, Bolshevik authorities had opened the party and Soviet organizations to the *jadids*, militant intellectual-nationalists, who were in many cases hostile to the Russians and sympathetic to the Basmachis. These men were not purged until 1932-38.

Stage 2, the period of rapid social transformation, complete collectivization, secularization of education and the courts, the increasing pressure against Islam, and the liquidation of remaining pre-revolutionary intellectuals began in the late 1920s and ended with World War II.

The groups of people who fled across the Soviet borders from 1917-1939 likewise may be divided into two groups which are delimited by two sets of socio-historical factors. Initially Basmachi sympathizers, dispossessed peasants and victims of famine from the countryside formed the majority of those seeking refuge in Afghanistan and Chinese Turkestan. Many of these people returned to the Soviet Union when the war-related disruption was over. Those who remained in Afghanistan settled in villages to become farmers as they had been before. They retained tribal names by which they identified themselves.

After 1928, those who crossed the border were primarily from a more urbanized population. These people moved into Afghan towns near the border; they did not seek to become landowners. While the collectivization campaign may have played some role in convincing these people to leave, their own view is that they left for the sake of maintaining their religious traditions. As one old man said, "As a boy one day the police stopped me on the way to the mosque and took me to the station. I couldn't stand the life there anymore." These are the people who took the title of *muhajirs*. The fact that the campaign against Islam, "the complete disintegration of Muslim society," began only after 1928 supports the contention that ideological conviction played an important role in determining these last emigrants (Bennigsen 1967:165).[1]

23

An independent source reported in the late 1930s again demonstrates the characteristics of the latter group of emigrants. Ahmad Jan, age 20, from the village of Qilich near Kasan met the traveller/researcher Gunnar Jarring in Kashmir in 1934. He had spent some time in Afghanistan en route. Though a farmer himself, his father was a mullah who five years earlier "had left his native country owing to the persecution of the Mohammadan clergy by the anti-religious leagues (1937b:23).

The stories of the journeys across the border were not frequently talked about. Children born in Afghanistan often did not know the details of their parents' former lives. One colorful story described the pitfalls of the long road to the place of refuge. It also demonstrated concern with Islamic observance. This was the story of a man named Haji Omar,[2] a failed bootmaker, who was not especially prominent in his community but who did see five sons reach adulthood. He also gave permission for an American anthropologist to live with his family.

> In his youth over 40 years ago, my father decided to cross the border into Afghanistan. Since his parents had died when he was a small child, he told his only living relative, a sister, who was married with two young children, that he would return although that was not his intention. He joined a group of ten travelling to the border, first using the main well-travelled routes and later, walking by night and sleeping by day far out in the steppe. Everyone's possessions were loaded on one donkey. Near the Amu, the company ran out of food and my father was sent to the nearest village for bread. In order to reach the village, he was forced to ford a large stream. No sooner had he arrived at the village when it began to rain. The stream became impassable and my father was unable to return with the food for four days. In the meantime, as it was a matter of life and death, the people decided to kill and eat the donkey's forbidden meat. Just as they had finished a hearty meal, my father returned with the bread. Everyone then was guilty of the sin of eating unlawful meat since it was no longer a matter of life and death. One man was so angry at my father that he threatened to kill him unless he too would eat the donkey meat. Since there was bread available, he refused. The other members of the group supported him and he was not forced to eat the meat. All these travellers settled in Kunduz where the one man maintained his anger and refused to speak to my father for at least ten years.

There were many ways to reach Afghanistan. The Soviets began many new collective farms in sparsely settled regions. Many people volunteered for the new settlements along the Amu Darya *dasht* (steppe) in the hopes of finding the way to

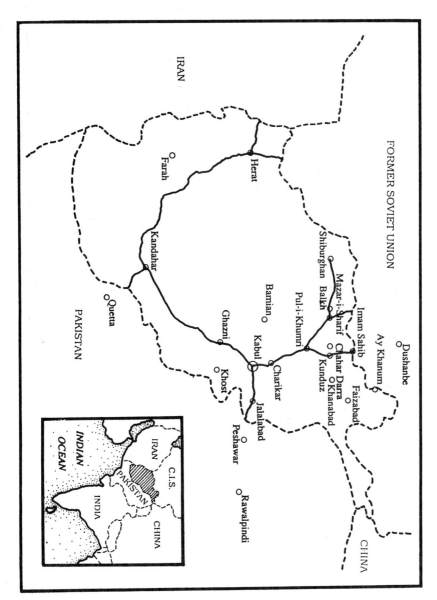

MAP 3.1 - AFGHANISTAN TOWNS

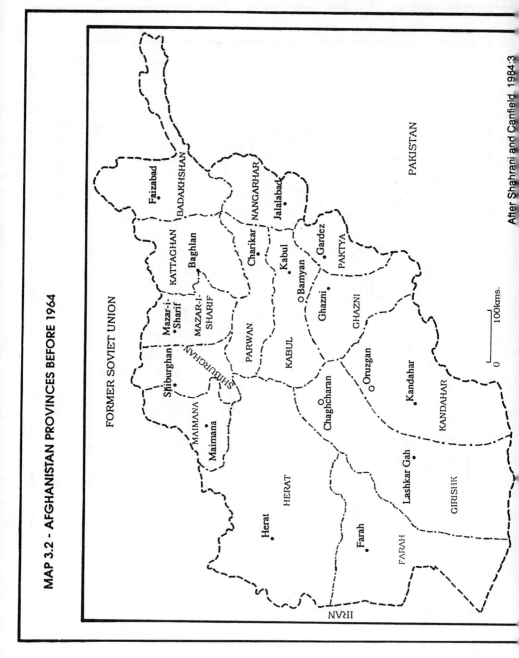

MAP 3.2 - AFGHANISTAN PROVINCES BEFORE 1964

After Shahrani and Canfield. 1984:3

slip across the border. In these new farms, men from the same towns or neighboring regions became friends, recognizing each other through speech pattern, dress, and asking about mutual acquaintance and kin; and some then decided to slip across the border together. Crossing the Amu by boat, they reached towns just on the Afghan side of the border. One of the major ports of entry was the town of Imam Sahib (also called Qizil Qala and now Shir Khan Bandar) which consisted of a bazaar of about 100 shops and about 200 households (Kushkeki 1926:46). From there many went to Khanabad, then the capital of Kattagan province and the seat of the governor. As the administrative center, Khanabad town contained 744 households, 394 shops and 19 caravanserais (Kushkeki 1926:18). Both of these towns still contained *muhajirs* in the mid 1970s. (For the location of these towns, see Map 3.1 and for the location of the provinces, including Kattagan, as they existed before 1964, see Map 3.2.)

While the *muhajirs* may have hoped to have support from the Afghan government, such was not the case by the 1930s. King Amanullah had been known for his support of the Basmachis and other Pan-Islamic movements in the early years of his reign, especially from 1919 to 1922, but he later instituted a policy of appeasement toward the British and Soviets, thereby alienating much of the population of Afghan Turkestan (Shahrani 1986: 46-56). Habibullah II, a Tajik, (known as Bacha-i Saqaw) who overthrew Amanullah gained much popularity in Afghan Turkestan for his anti-Soviet policies but was not able to prevent Nadir Shah, with European financial assistance and his army of tribal Pashtuns, from taking the throne. Nadir Shah instituted the policy of ethnic politics and extreme Pashtun favoritism which marked the Musahiban dynasty from that point on.[3] For example, thousands of Pashtuns from the East and South of Afghanistan were encouraged by the government to move to the Kunduz area as it became the target for economic development and much land was alienated from the original Uzbek inhabitants. It was this situation which confronted the *muhajirs* as they entered Afghanistan in the 1930s.

The government's economic development hopes for Kunduz were based on cotton. In 1925 a Pashtun, Abdul Aziz, discovered that the Soviet Union needed cotton, at least partially because of the economic chaos in Central Asia described above. Realizing that Kattagan had a similar climate to the best cotton lands in Central Asia, he bought up land in the Kunduz area which he cleared, drained and planted with cotton. His success convinced others to participate in this effort (including Bank-i Milli) and thus the Spinzar company was formed. The name is Pashto and means "white gold." The conversion of swampland to one of the most agriculturally productive areas in Afghanistan was aided by Nadir Shah, who after ridding himself of Habibullah II, taking the throne and discovering an empty treasury, forceably induced many Pashtun landlords to buy land in the area at about a dollar an acre (N. Dupree 1967:101-102). The governor of Kattagan, Shir Khan Nashir, supported the Spinzar Company and decided to move his capital to Kunduz where he decided to build an entirely new town with planned streets and marketplace.

Though Kunduz had been an important town since the thirteenth century and was something of a capital of Afghan Turkestan in the nineteenth when its ruler, Murad Beg, was the chieftain of the North, its population was constantly depleted by endemic malaria. Even in the nineteenth century, Kunduz had perhaps only 500 households (Wood 1872:138), a number that did not increase by the 1920s (Kushkeki 1926:51). In the early 1930s, the English explorer and adventurer Robert Byron wrote in his diary when forced to stop at Kunduz that "Even before leaving Teheran, we had resolved not to sleep at Kunduz if we could help it. Moorcroft died of fever caught in these marshes. There is a proverb which says a visit to Kunduz is tantamount to suicide. Here we are therefore lying in a mulberry grove beside a stagnant pool, both irresistible attractions to the fatal mosquito" (1937:260). Byron also reported on the power of the governor Shir Khan, who was an impressive domineering man. Apparently between Khanabad and Kunduz there was a truck accident on the bridge over the river. "Now the Governor of Kunduz rode up on a fast grey pacer, an angry red-bearded man, who set about the population with his whip, bidding them haul the lorry out and mend the bridge before morning" (263).

In 1935, Gunnar Jarring visited the new Kunduz after a three-day, three hundred mile truck journey from Kabul.

> Shir Khan now ordered a town to be constructed in the place of the old, and in a short time there grew up not less than 900 shops and 14 large inns and caravanserais at the place indicated by the governor. A new built road fit for motor traffic between Khanabad and Mazar-i Sharif runs through the town . . . In the centre of the town there is a large circular market from which the different streets run out. The streets are furnished with pavements and also simple but satisfactory drainage. Traders had already occupied some of the shops (November 1935) and I suppose the new town of Kunduz is quite finished now (Jarring 1937a:144-145).

The growth of the new Kunduz attracted many *muhajirs* from Khanabad. They bought shops in the new bazaar and were able to acquire prime locations. The central circle mentioned by Jarring contained the *chapan*-selling shops and each of these 25+ was still owned by a *muhajir* in the 1970s.[4] At first, many Ferghanachis lived on bandar-i Khanabad, the section of town on the way to Khanabad. While there, three men from Kasan decided to form their own *mahalla* or neighborhood.

After surveying the grassland surrounding new Kunduz, the Kasanis decided on a particular area near a canal owned by a kinsman of Shir Khan. Reluctant to sell his pasture, this man dismissed the Kasanis with an offer to sell at 1000 Afghanis per *jerib*. This price was about 5 times the going rate but to the man's surprise, the Kasanis, though somewhat resentful, realized that given the political situation, they could not do better, and therefore agreed to the first price and bought 14 *jeribs* for their neighborhood. The founders still held the original land deed in the early 1980s when some households were confiscated by local representatives of the Marxist government.

## Kunduz Before the Marxist Coup

Through the years after Shir Khan's building of the new Kunduz, the town and the region assumed increasing national importance. With Soviet aid, the port on the Amu Darya, Imam Sahib, was modernized and renamed Shir Khan Bandar. The route from Shir Khan Bandar through Kunduz to Kabul became the major transportation route for the Soviet-Afghan import-export trade. The paving of this route was completed in 1964 and the trip which had taken several weeks when the Hindu Kush mountain passes were snowed in then took only six to eight hours.

During most winters in the 1970s, the Salang pass through the Hindu Kush was closed only for a few days; apart from these there were no major halts in the transportation of goods and people from one side of the Hindu Kush to the other. An inhabitant of Kunduz could reach Kabul via several bus and minibus services, and there were bi-weekly flights to Kabul via twin-engine airplanes owned by Afghanistan's domestic air service (Canfield 1989: 16).

The ease of transportation drew the *muhajir* communities of Imam Sahib, Khanabad, Kunduz, Baghlan and Kabul together.[5] *(See Map 3.1)* There was frequent visiting by both men and women. Even the trip to Kabul held no barrier for women. Though *muhajir* women did not usually ride buses or planes, private taxis were hired or cars borrowed. Accompanied by a male relative seated by the driver, groups of women journeyed to and from towns for weddings and circumcision parties, staying with relatives for weeks at a time.

In addition to its role in cotton production and as a transportation center, Kunduz also gained national significance because of its location in one of the most well-watered valley regions of Afghanistan. The 300 mile Kunduz river is one of the two tributaries of the Amu Darya in Afghanistan. Kunduz was second only to Balkh province in the amount of land under irrigation and was therefore the center for rice production along with fruits and vegetables sent all over Afghanistan. A 1950s development study compared cotton production in the Kunduz region with the United States, the Soviet Union, Egypt, Pakistan and India and indicated that Kunduz produced close to the US and Soviet average reported yield per acre and surpassed Pakistan and India. Problems preventing greater yield included undependable water supply, limited amount of irrigable land, competition with grain crops and possible labor shortage (Michel 1959:301-302). Also important in Kunduz province was karakul sheep production, which probably developed in Bukhara and was brought south by pastoralists. Karakul sheep production depends on short range nomadism and good quality and quantity of feed for ewes (Michel 1959: 334-335).

The ethnic mix which constituted the town was constantly renewed. The fertility of the Kunduz hinterland had a definite impact on the lives of the urban dwellers. Kunduz became a magnet in times of famine as in the early 1970s for those in need of food and work. Agricultural production contributed to the abundance of the seasonal food supply in the town bazaar and the daily diet of inhabitants. Within the town itself, many had gardens with fruit trees and flowers, the products of which were kept for home use and given to neighbors.

The staple diet of most people in Afghanistan was bread and rice. The Kunduz region was self-sufficient in both. Potatoes, carrots, black-eyed peas, mung beans, chick peas and onions were available throughout the year but many vegetables and fruits were available only after local harvest. These were: squash, fall; spinach, early spring; turnips, November-January; lettuce, late March-early April; cucumber, late May-early June; tomato, spring and fall; eggplant, late spring; okra, late spring; apricot, late spring; pear varieties, fall; apple varieties, June-December; peach varieties, June-November; mulberry varieties, April-June; almond, July; quince, October; plum, May-July; grape, June-December; melon, July-December; watermelon, August-January; fig, June. Citrus fruits did not grow in the Kunduz area and were brought in from Jalalabad in eastern Afghanistan.

Many Kunduzis kept either cows or sheep in sheds in the household compounds. Among the Ferghanachis cows were most frequently kept. Many of the wealthier households had as many as five cows, but usually there were only two or three. During the spring calving season, the diet was therefore enriched by milk, cream, butter, or yogurt nearly every day. Generally, the households with an excess of milk products sold to neighbors or to neighborhood food shops and gained additional income. Animals were not raised for slaughter. Since Islam requires only animals slaughtered by slitting the throats as appropriate for food, meat was bought in the marketplace when needed, and sick, old or infirm animals were sold to butchers.

Because of Shir Khan's planning, it was easy to learn the locations of various shops and neighborhoods in Kunduz. The four main routes through the town met in the central circle. These streets retained the old names as if they were gates enclosing a walled town (Figure 3.1). They were bandar-i Imam Sahib, bandar-i Khanabad, bandar-i Kabul and bandar-i Hukumati, the latter passing the

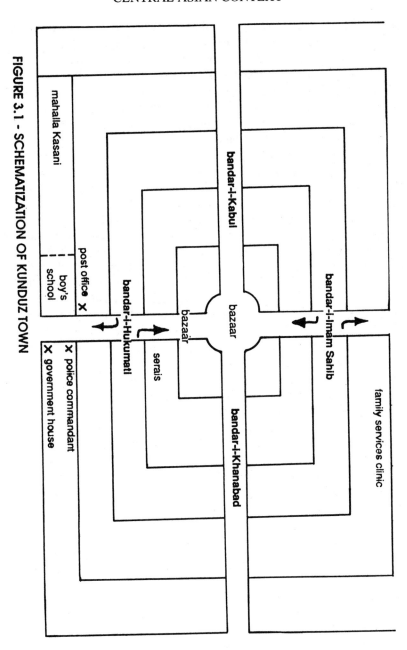

FIGURE 3.1 - SCHEMATIZATION OF KUNDUZ TOWN

government buildings. The town was laid out in even squares which surrounded the center circle. The center circle and the first square comprised the major bazaar area. The second square contained many areas which serviced caravans and other transport. Though shops continued along the four main roads, other areas beyond the second square were primarily private walled household compounds.

The Kunduz bazaar like other Afghan town bazaars and central Asian bazaars in the 19th century contained shops selling the same product or service grouped together along the same lane. There were over forty services and occupations represented in the bazaar. These included: bread bakers, hardware, rubber shoe sales, barbers, carpet/karakul sales, bathhouses, teahouses, pharmacies with western medicines, *tabibs* (doctors) with traditional medicine, fish sales, bicycle repairs, tinsmithing, blacksmithing, cotton sales, handwoven textile sales, china sales, dried fruits/nuts, pottery, straw mats, coal, poplar poles, butchers, placed vegetables, used western clothing, *chapan*/embroidered hat, wool and animal hides, grain, candy makers and sales, textile merchants, carpenters, lumber, jewelry makers, coppersmithing, salt, burlap bag, rice, sewing supplies, chicken, horsecart repair, radio repair and general grocery. The Ferghanachis controlled four occupations: tinsmithing, *chapan* selling, hardware and burlap bag sales. *Chapan* selling was probably introduced by the *muhajirs* in the Kattagan area. Not only do informants believe that they introduced the wearing of the *chapan* in the area, but Slobin also has reported that *chapan* sales in Mazar-i-Sharif are dominated by emigrants who arrived around 1932 (1976:17).

Other occupations in which *muhajirs* participated were radio repair, sewing supplies, barbers and textile sales. In these they numbered about one-third of the total participants. There were also occupations associated with tribal Uzbeks and other ethnic groups. Thus Qungrats owned shops which sold cotton husks and along with the Lakai, pottery shops. Other Uzbeks made special candy and sold handmade textiles.

The basic construction, structure and function of the household compound and neighborhood institutions changed little in the 20th century. Bacon defined many of the functions of the Central Asian *mahalla* (neighborhood) and its socio-political structure.

> The ward was a close-knit community governed by a council of elders. An outsider could not buy a house in the ward without the permission of the community. The mosque was for the use of all male residents as well as the rooms where men warmed water in winter for ablutions preceding early morning prayer. Large kettles were also kept in these rooms for cooking *pilaw* for family or community festivals. All the residents contributed to the maintenance of these rooms and of the water

channel that ran through the ward . . . Families of the ward helped each other with their family celebrations--circumcisions, weddings, funerals-- and joined in celebrating religious festivals (1966:73).

Despite the disruption of their previous life, the *Ferghanachis* continued the *mahalla* form of urban organization in Kunduz. In addition to the small Kasani neighborhood, most Ferghanachis lived in the larger Namangani neighborhood on the other side of Kunduz. Although parts of Kunduz did not contain *mahallas* founded by various ethnic groups, there was still a tendency for co-ethnics to live nearby, a practice that reinforced group solidarity where ethnic groups were small. Thus, even the Kazakhs were integrated into a neighborhood also home to many *muhajir* Uzbeks and Tajiks and the Hindus also had a neighborhood. Areas known as *mahallas* lacked surrounding walls and a single gate for the entire area. Instead, there was a series of interlocked lanes; each lane, *kocha*, had a wooden gate which was locked by its inhabitants at night from the inside. In the Kasani neighborhood only three or four household compounds were found along each *kocha*. Doorways were cut into compound walls so that women could visit each other without walking in the frequently travelled *kocha*. A woman was thus able to visit the immediately adjacent neighbor without veiling and could visit a nearby household while veiled with her face uncovered.

The original buyers of the land that became *mahalla* Kasani sold off portions to other Kasanis and *muhajirs* through the years. Land had increasingly been subdivided, enclosed in walls and sold or rented to outsiders. For example, when one man needed money for the marriage of a son, he mortgaged (made a *giraw* contract for) the middle compound of the three he owned to an Andkhoi Uzbek family for 20,000 Afghanis. He also rented one compound to an Arab family for 600 afghanis per month, a relatively low rent for the area (See Barfield 1981 on the Arab ethnic group). A Pashtun family who lived immediately behind the Arabs in the next *kocha* paid 1,200 afs/month for rent. One of the man's sons estimated that they could sell their household compounds for 200,000 afs because of their excellent location near a major canal.

There were about 60 household compounds within *mahalla* Kasani. In addition to the 15 Kasani households, there were 14 *muhajir* Uzbek and 5 *muhajir* Tajik households. These 34 households together constituted the core community of the *mahalla*. Of the other 26 households, there were five Pashtun households including one renter; two Badakhshani Tajik households; four Panjshiri Tajik households, one Andkhoi Uzbek household, one Chahar Darra Tajik household, one Arab household; one Hindu household; two Kabuli households and nine households rented to various Tajiks with fairly rapid turnover so that social relationships between these families and the permanent residents did not develop.

*Photo 3.1 Animal Bazaar Near Kunduz*

The heterogeneous composition of the neighborhood should not be viewed as innovative since Central Asia cities traditionally contained both ethnically mixed and ethnically uniform neighborhoods (Bacon 1966:73). In any case, the overwhelming amount of daily interaction occurred only between members of the *mahalla*'s core community. Community and kin relationships were defined by Islamic ideals of the *umma*, the early community of the faithful who took care of widows, orphans and the poor. Life crisis rituals such as circumcision celebrations, marriages and deaths were also based in neighborhood and community cooperation and reinforced the Islamic ambience of everyday life (Canfield 1985: 62-63).

## NOTES

1. Another confirmation of the time period in which the last wave of emigration took place was that many informants remembered hearing about or learning the latin alphabet that was officially adopted in 1928 but only one knew the Cyrillic alphabet adopted in 1940.

2. When discussing material to be included in this book with informants, I asked about the use of real names, pseudonyms, and initials. They suggested that when information indicated a person's honor after his death that his real name be used, but when information did not indicate honor that the name not be used. They also preferred that living people not be referred to by name. I therefore use initials for the living and for those who would be hurt if names were used.

3. The government made Pashto the official language of Afghanistan in 1936. It was not until the Constitution of 1964 that Dari, Afghan Persian, was also made an official language.

4. According to informants, three shops were considered to belong to Badakhshanis. The owners were actually *muhajirs* who settled in a village in Badakhshan. Because they were isolated from the community for a long time, they were considered outsiders and village Tajiks. These men had been involved in the manufacture of *chapan* cloth and bought into sales through an intermediary.

5. The Kabul area was dependent on Kunduz-Baghlan for several commodities including cotton, sugar, rice, and wheat. The regime sought to maintain its political control of northern Afghanistan through these economic and infrastructural linkages. However, the development of the Salang pass allowed for greater Soviet economic penetration. See Michel 1959:394-395.

# Part II

The Ferghanachis in Kunduz Before 1978

# Chapter 4

# The Household

Since I went to Afghanistan in 1976 intending to study village Uzbeks either in Jawzjan or Balkh provinces, I was not prepared for the urban milieu of Kunduz. Because of the multi-ethnic nature of the town and its neighborhoods, I was forced to adapt and use network analysis, relying on the family with whom I lived for introductions to neighbors, kin, and other members of their ethnic group. Unlike most ethnographers who first conduct a village or neighborhood census, as a single unaccompanied foreign woman in a Islamic society, my knocking on the doors of strangers' households was not appropriate nor was it safe. I had to delay gaining family census material until I could meet the women of each household in other contexts and then was invited by them to meet their menfolk.

Despite these difficulties, I was privileged in several ways. Through a special arrangement by the Ministry of Education, I was permitted to live with a Kunduz family, the very Ferghanachi joint family whom I had met through John Summers of the Afghan-American Educational Commission. This was at a time when foreigners were not even supposed to visit Afghans in their homes without special approval. Since only one person in the family knew English and he was gone for several months of the year, I had to communicate using my limited knowledge of Persian and Uzbek which I had studied at Harvard. The family was not wealthy and I had to quickly adjust to the lack of western-style bathrooms and plumbing in addition to sleeping on a mat in the same room with at least two other adults and four children and sometimes others. I had to learn how to eat rice by scooping it with my fingers and not allowing it to spill all over the floor. When visitors came I was there and when the women of the household went to visit others or attended a celebration, I went, too. I therefore was completely immersed in the field situation and was in the vortex of a household's daily routine without even trying. I paid a monthly sum for rent, food, and for the general assistance provided by this family.

This field situation differed from those of other women ethnographers in Afghanistan of the 1970s. Mills, for example, though a single woman like me, had her own household and was in the early stages of her fieldwork accompanied by an interpreter and a government representative (1991:3-10). Tapper was married; though she and her husband initially set up their own small household, they also lived in the guesthouse of a prominent tribal man (1991:7). Thus she felt the lack of privacy as I did, but as a married woman was not as anomalous.

Mills has reported that the storytellers she was recording early in her research and their audience knew that her language skills in the Herati dialect of Persian were inadequate and used that knowledge accordingly (1991:14). The Ferghanachi field situation was also fraught with linguistic problems because the people were

39

fluent bilinguals and it was quite possible that they would use Uzbek as a secret language because my ability to speak Uzbek was even worse than my ability in Afghan Persian. By a fortuitous circumstance, people became convinced that I was equally fluent in both languages and they did not then choose one over the other. I had brought a collection of Uzbek language folktales from Andkhoi recorded by Gunnar Jarring in the 1930s written in latin script (Jarring 1938). One evening shortly after I had moved in with the family, I took out the collection to show it and began to read it aloud to them. I could read Uzbek! This created a sensation in the neighborhood. Ethnographers are given many roles by the people they study and this collection of Uzbek stories was the beginning of my entertainment role. On visits I was requested to bring the book so I could entertain the women. If I neglected to take it I was even sent back to get it. The women preferred the more salacious stories, especially one of attempted seduction of a virtuous girl who is rewarded with marriage to a prince. Though I was uncomfortable at being the center of attention in this way and worried that I was preventing more typical events and conversations from happening, I eventually realized that this was part

*Photo 4. 1  The Ethnographer and an Informant Making Sumulak.*

of the reciprocity that must occur in fieldwork. The entertainment role also came to include my singing of "Happy Birthday" in English on appropriate occasions and my dancing Uzbek style at women's celebrations, both of which were a source of much amusement.

As an unmarried woman within a household, its members, especially the grandfather, took on the role of my protectors. For the most part they did not want me to go anywhere unaccompanied by either the women or a man. The grandfather only reluctantly allowed me to go to the public bath and this was the only place outside of the Ferghanachi neighborhoods that I went on a weekly basis. Visiting people of other ethnic groups was considered to be particularly dangerous because the men in those groups were not trustworthy. On one occasion, a Pashtun family in the next lane invited me to visit them. Only upon the assurance that they were a household composed of a widow and her children did the grandfather allow me to go. He also personally accompanied me home that day. A male informant accompanied me to the marketplace, the animal bazaar, and *buzkashi*, the horseback sporting event. I went other places when the women were going anyway, the cemetery, the family clinic, the hospital. In other words, the people did their best to assimilate me to a daughter of the household role with appropriate circumspect and modest demeanor. I did not generally veil because most of the time I was within someone's household. However, I did dress modestly with a dress over slacks and my head covered with a scarf. The grandfather frequently admonished me when my dress or tunic failed to reach my knees.

I did not realize until well into my fieldwork that the majority of people, including the mosque elders, had opposed my living in their community. There were several reasons for their feelings. They did not trust anyone who seemed to be from the government and I had had to obtain governmental permissions. They distrusted foreigners either as spies or because they did not understand why a foreigner would want to be with them. They knew about and despised young foreigners who traveled to Afghanistan at that time for drugs. They viewed foreign women as promiscuous and disruptive to the social order. All these attitudes I had to live down without knowing it because, of course, once I was there, hospitality and politeness meant these could not be mentioned. Because I was interested in the lives of women and children, and because I either stayed in the household or accompanied women in their ordinary routines, I gradually was perceived as non-threatening. The mosque leaders often greeted me when I accompanied a male informant on neighborhood streets. Finally near the end of fieldwork as I prepared to return to Kabul, I received a breakfast invitation from the most important religious authority of the neighborhood mosque. Though I had been to his house many times for visits and celebrations, he himself had not been present. On this occasion, he wanted a favor, which was that I photograph his family all together in the flower garden. He sat with me, ate with me, and talked to me as the others began their daily chores. I had achieved as much acceptance as any foreigner could.

From shortly after the Marxist coup to 1984, I was out of touch with the Ferghanachi community. Finally, the family with whom I had lived went to Pakistan and we were able to reestablish contact. The family later came to the United States. Because of my fieldwork from 1976-1977 and the contacts that developed from 1984, in studying the Ferghanachis in Pakistan in 1990, I did not have to start from the beginning. I lived with a family in Karachi whom I had known in Kunduz previously. Many of the women that I met during wedding celebrations and at social gatherings reminded me where and when they had seen me before. Though I did not bring the book of Uzbek tales and many wished I had, my presence alone elicited some tears and much nostalgia.

### Daily Life

For the Ferghanachi households of Kunduz, the sun's position determined the various divisions of the day, each of the five parts marked by specific prayer requirements. As the sun's position changed over the year, so too did the times allotted to the five divisions of the day. Thus the evening meal in summer was eaten at perhaps nine o'clock, while in the winter, it was eaten at five. Despite the shortening and lengthening of daylight hours during which household tasks were performed, the daily routine followed the same pattern throughout the year.

At daybreak or before the first call to prayer, everyone rose, used the bathroom shed, and performed the necessary cleanliness and purification rituals. Usually, the women began to sweep out the household courtyard, and put away the sleeping materials. Men fetched water from the canal which ran through the neighborhood. Water was kept in large tin storage tanks in the courtyard. Women began bread baking and sewing tasks, putting them aside to spread out the morning meal. In spring, women milked the cows and prepared milk by boiling it, and made butter or clotted cream for the meal. After the meal, men left for their shops in the bazaar. Married men occasionally helped their wives tend the livestock, but most of their work within the household compound involved repair, plastering the roof and walls, carpentry, gardening, and construction work.

The second meal of the day was frequently identical to the first; tea and bread were eaten regularly. In the winter, a rice dish might have been eaten at the mid-day and evening meals, but in the summer the evening meal was more likely to be a thick bean soup with yogurt. Men returned from the shops for the mid-day meal, or they ate in their shops after buying food in the bazaar. The entire family usually

*Photo 4.2 Animal Care*

*Photo 4.3 Division of Labor in the Household*

ate the evening meal together. A separate platter was given to children, but adults ate from the same platter. Etiquette dictated that an individual take rice from that part of the platter immediately in front of him.

During the afternoon women often visited neighbors for tea and gossip, taking along sewing or embroidery work. In the summer's heat, there was usually time for a nap after the mid-day meal. Toward evening the livestock would again be cared for, cows milked and led back to the shed. Before the meal, the same tasks as in the early morning were repeated. Women swept out the courtyard. Men brought water from the canal and watered down the dust of the courtyard. Many men made a practice of attending the mosque every evening before the meal.

Soon after the meal, sleeping mats, pillows, and blankets were laid down. The children went to sleep and especially in winter they were quickly joined by the adults. In summer, everyone slept on the veranda, or on small wooden bed frames in the yard; unmarried men slept on the roof. In winter, the individual sleeping mats were grouped around the *sandali*, a recessed firepit in the floor. Everyone always slept fully dressed. These daily activities took for granted a basic landscape, the areas inside and outside the walled household compound, and material culture, food, clothing and shelter.

By the 1970s, some of the houses within the compound walls of *mahalla* Kasani had been in continual use for over forty years. These houses and their additions were constructed in the pattern which was the most common in Afghanistan and Central Asia. They were square or rectangular and made of sun-dried brick covered with a mud and straw plaster. The bricks were made in molds, and dried on the ground. Flat roofs of earth and straw were supported on poplar poles covered by straw matting. In winter, snow was shoveled off the roofs and nearly every fall, the roofs were re-plastered so they did not leak. Workers were hired in the bazaar to make the bricks or mud plaster right from the mud in the compound courtyard. The household compound usually included storage sheds, animal pens, cooking areas, a courtyard area for family work and children's play, and a small pool, or *juy* (small canal). The basic structure was the same as described by Bacon for the traditional Central Asian urban pattern.

> The house itself was oriented toward the courtyard; on that side, the house walls were punctuated by open work plaster grills or wooden doors which were usually kept open in summer for ventilation and light. Also facing the courtyard was a roofed veranda which protected the rooms from the direct rays of the summer sun. Extending beyond the veranda was a baked clay terrace, the *aivan*. In the courtyard, a bread oven stood near the kitchen; in a corner where two walls met was a toilet; and along one or more walls were stalls for

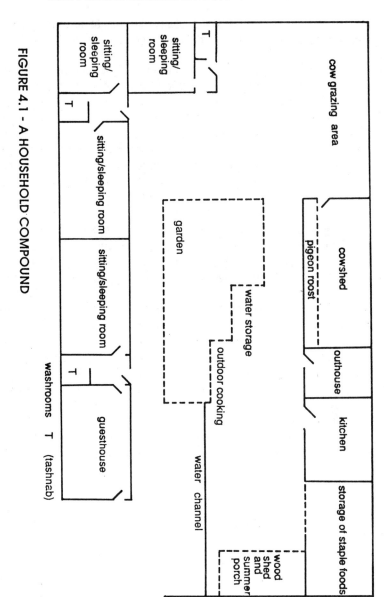

FIGURE 4.1 - A HOUSEHOLD COMPOUND

animals. . . . In the suburbs and in the country, the walls of the courtyard were extended to embrace a vegetable garden and fruit orchards (1966:61).

In the Ferghanachi houses of Kunduz, glass windows that opened on the courtyard had replaced the plaster grill and wooden doors described by Bacon.

Each sitting/sleeping room facing the courtyard was a separate house (*khana*--Persian; *ui*--Uzbek) in local view. Thus, one heard references to Mahmuda's houses, Hanifa's house within the same compound. Interior houses were always referred to as the property of women. When a male informant described his living situation he said, "My mother gave my wife these two houses when we had two children." The houses were his mother's and then they became his wife's. Only the guesthouse, *mehmankhana*, and the land itself were seen as male property. Women could also own land though inheritance.

The pattern shown in Figure 4.1 indicates a simplification of traditional compound structure. According to Zhilina, the traditional Uzbek household structure in Khorezm north of the Amu Darya was clear in its division into two halves--the external, male half often including several guesthouses, livestock and feed barns, workshops, and a courtyard; and the female half which included dwelling rooms, storerooms, the kitchen, verandas for sleeping in summer, and another courtyard. She reports that the "entire life of the family took place in the female half" (1974:66). The difference between the compound structure Zhilina described and the pattern used in Kunduz was probably based on class and rural versus urban difference. Bacon (1966) and Meakin (1908:646-47) likewise describe a traditional two courtyard pattern, but Bacon specifies that more modest homes contained only the *mehmankhana*. Households too small for a strict division between *tashkar*, external, male areas, and *ishkar*, interior, female areas, did away with the male side. Urban compounds were probably smaller than rural ones because urban land was more expensive and higher population required more intensive use of space.

Most of the Ferghanachi households contained only the *mehmankhana* with all other structures hidden in the interior courtyard. Even the few households which were large enough to contain two courtyards had all other structures, with the exceptions of the guesthouses, located in the interior courtyard. Only the Kasani community leaders who lived near the mosque and studyhouse (*qarikhana*) had households of the two courtyard pattern.

Household furnishings were fairly simple. Straw matting was laid on the mud floors and over this were spread woven rugs called *gilam* (English--kilims), or more rarely, felt rugs or Turkmen carpets. The latter were most often used in the rooms where guests were received. Niches in the walls held teapots and household articles, stacks of hand-sewn cotton comforters, sleeping mats and pillows. In winter, a *sandali* was used to provide warmth in most rooms. The *sandali* was constructed by placing a low wooden table over a recess built into the mud floor. The recess was filled with ashes from outside cooking fires; the table was covered by several quilts hanging down all four sides; and people sat or slept with legs and parts of their bodies under the quilts. When the *sandali* was in use, food was served on its table, a custom that apparently dates from Bukhara or Tashkent in the nineteenth century (Bacon 1966:62). Usually, a cloth was spread on the floor for meals. *Bukharis*, wood-burning stoves, were also common. However, in many households they were used only when guests were present because of the prohibitive expense of wood.

In addition to large iron cooking pots, the kitchen shed contained knives, wooden soup spoons, bowls, and platters. Grains and other dry staples were stored in clay jars or burlap bags held in wooden boxes. In summer, cooking was done outside and in winter in the shed where a kind of low platform made of clay, with fire pits fed from openings in the side was built. Cooking pots were placed over holes in the top of the earthen stove. Pieces of wood, brush, and dried dung patties made from animal manure were used for fuel. Flat circular bread was baked in barrel-shaped ovens of clay. A brush fire was lit within the oven and allowed to burn out. Then thirty or more pieces of dough were plastered onto the oven walls to bake. A woman made bread three or four times a week.

During the early Soviet period in Central Asia, three additional pieces of furniture that became great prestige items were bookcases, wardrobes for clothing, and buffets or cabinets for dishes (Bacon 1966:163). These items were still highly valued as of the 1970s. The *mehmankhana* in Haji Omar's household contained the family's only bookcase and wooden wardrobe. The wardrobe contained no clothing; clothing was actually stored in decorated metal trunks in other sleeping rooms. Both of Omar's daughters-in-law received cabinets for their dishes as part of their bridegifts. These cabinets were placed in the wall niches of their respective houses. All household articles like the sleeping rooms themselves belonged to women.

To demonstrate the range of personal possessions that a newly married woman expected in her new home, I surveyed the belongings of the brides in the *mahalla*. A typical list contained: straw matting, two *gilams*, one carpet, one *sandali* table, two other small tables, one *charpayi* (wooden bed frame), several metal trunks, a cassette player-radio, four prayer cloths, five sheets, five curtains, twelve pillows, five sleeping mats, five quilts, one hand-cranked sewing machine, two mirrors, four tablecloths, ten hand towels, five face cloths, four large teapots, two small teapots, twenty teacups, ten large glasses, twelve bowls, thirty small plates, twelve platters, a water storage container, and two water pitchers for use in the washroom and for washing hands before meals.

Though men's and women's clothing differed slightly in form, their basic structure was the same and the same terminology was used. A shirt was called *pirahan* (Persian) or *koinak* (Uzbek), and trousers were called *tomban* (Persian) or *ishtan* (Uzbek).

The typical man's shirt worn throughout the North had no collar; its opening on one shoulder was closed by a button. The shirt reached to the knees and was slit up each side for ease of sitting. The shirt hung outside trousers which were perhaps six feet wide at the waist and were pulled in by a drawstring. White was the color most often worn by old men, but younger men frequently wore shades of blue or gray. Enough cloth was bought in the bazaar for a *koinak* and *ishtan* to be sewn of the same material. Adult men wore a loose open quilted coat of either striped cotton or cotton and silk cloth. These *chapan* (Persian) or *ton* (Uzbek) were constructed with overlong sleeves and when folded became triangular. In this folded condition, they were occasionally used as prayer cloths. I was told that the Quran prohibits the use of pure silk for men. Therefore *chapans* always contained some cotton fiber. (Schuyler 1877, I:190 also reports this). All ethnic groups including Pashtuns wore the *chapan* in northern Afghanistan. Even newcomers from Kabul working in modern sector occupations usually bought at least one *chapan*.

Formerly, all Ferghanachi men and boys shaved their heads. This practice had disappeared among men in their twenties through forties by the 1970s. Shaven heads were said to facilitate purification; the scalp became wet even when washed rapidly. Young boys and often young girls had their heads shaved in winter for hygienic reasons. A young man told me that Uzbek barbers were the best if one wanted a shaven head. Since he preferred to keep his hair, he went to a Tajik.

All men and boys wore embroidered caps. These caps were distinctive as to ethnic group and origin. Members of all ethnic groups were immediately able to place strangers in ethnic slots by glancing at the caps. Dupree has mentioned some exchanging of headgear styles among neighboring village Uzbeks and Tajiks (1973:246). The Ferghanachi wore two styles of caps, black or green velvet backing with embroidered multi-colored flowers, and the same velvet backing with gold leaves. In the early 1970s, many young men began to wear caps sent to their families by relatives in Uzbekistan or brought back by visitors. These caps differed from others made in Afghanistan, and they were unquestionably a symbol of identification with fellow ethnics in the Soviet Union.

Old men, especially devout individuals, wore white turbans wound around their caps. Certain occupations or groups favored particular colors or materials as turban cloths. Informants were able to point out the types favored by gamblers and merchants. Ferghanachi elders tucked in the end-flap of the turban lowering the flap to shoulder length only to pray. In a custom which they associated with

Pashtuns, the flap was allowed to dangle at all times. I saw flaps of turbans dangling to waist length and beyond. Ferghanachi elders believed this was sacrilegious and deprecated the fact that many of their young men sought to follow this style.

Women's shirts were sewn of brightly colored material available in the bazaar. A little girl's shirt reached only to her hips; a young married woman's shirt usually reached her knees; women in their forties and fifties wore mid-calf to ankle-length dresses. Women were known for their sewing ability and were often hired by women of other ethnic groups to make dresses and children's clothes. I saw women known as noted seamstresses who constructed their own patterns following pictures in old American clothing catalogs. They cut pieces to a person's size using the hand measurements reported by Andreev in 1928 for Kasan (p. 124). Under women's *pirahan*, full trousers similar to the men's but of finer material were worn. White and pale pastels were favored as most suitable. Urban women of all groups bought synthetic laces in the bazaar and decorated the bottoms of their trousers. Ferghanachi women also used a distinctive band of inserted crochet-work near the bottom of the trousers. In Tsarist days, factory-woven velvet, velveteen and plush became favorites for women's jackets (Bacon 1966:165). This fashion continued to be popular and many older women wore black velvet jackets when visiting.

Little girls went bareheaded in the home especially if they had the traditional Uzbek hairstyle of forty or more tiny braids. More often, girls and young married women wore one long braid covered at all times by a kerchief (*chadar*--Persian, *rumal*--Uzbek), tied under the hair or left on the shoulders like a shawl. Older women usually had two braids with a longer white kerchief wrapped around their hair.

The veil (*chadari*--Persian, *paranji*--Uzbek) used by Ferghanachi women was also worn by all other urban women in Afghanistan. Often light blue or mustard colored, the pleated rayon garment was draped over the head and body and reached almost to the ground in back. An embroidered meshlike portion over the face enabled the wearer to see. The traditional two-piece *paranji* consisting of the horsehair face cover and the open coat was nowhere in evidence. The veil was first worn by girls around the age of puberty. Since girls were increasingly likely to attend school, the adoption of the veil was sometimes delayed until age fourteen or fifteen, or the girl went veiled to celebrations at night and wore her school uniform by day.

Girls did not use cosmetics until their wedding celebrations at which time friends assisted in its initial application. Western-style lipstick, face powder, and eye shadow were used. The traditional kohl, *sorma*, was used as eyeliner and was believed to cure eye inflammation. For this reason, it was put on new-born babies

*Photo 4.4 Man in turban*
*and chapan*

*Photo 4.5  Older woman*

*Photo 4.6  Veiled Women at buzkashi tournament.*

and young children every few days. Mothers also blackened girl babies' brows and the space between them into one long line. This was thought to encourage the growth of long thick black brows, a symbol of beauty. Occasionally, adolescent girls and married women also made up their eyebrows in this manner. Henna was applied to the hands for festivals and weddings. Despite the addition of western cosmetic products, ideas of beauty and the application of cosmetics adhered to traditional standards.

Town bazaars in Afghanistan contained special areas which sold second-hand clothing. The clothes, often in excellent condition, came primarily from the United States and Europe. Sweaters, jackets, coats, shoes, and sandals bought in the used-clothing bazaar were worn by Ferghanachis of all ages. Young men occasionally owned western-style shirts and trousers. School girls bought a blouse and skirt in the bazaar and wore the traditional *ishtan* underneath.

The used clothing business cut deeply into several traditional crafts. One never saw Uzbek shoes worn by Uzbeks; they were only sold to tourists. European shoes, Pakistani rubber sandals and plastic boots were worn in all towns. Western-style underwear for both sexes was beginning to be popular. The resulting appearance of most people had become an intriguing blend of traditional and modern, old and new, in alternating layers.

In addition to regular meals, tea and candies were always placed before guests. Before each meal, a child carried around a pitcher of water so that hands could be rinsed. If guests were present, a metal basin and towel were also carried to each guest. If only family was present, everyone rinsed hands before sitting down. Hands were washed again after eating. At a large gathering, the pitcher, basin, soap, and towels were carried around to the guests after the meal. Before each meal, the *bismulla* (In the name of God, the merciful and compassionate) was recited. After the meal, a member of the family recited a prayer of thanksgiving which everyone joined by saying the *amin,* amen.

The ritual aspect of each meal was extremely important. Bread was always placed with the top side up; it was broken and passed to diners, never cut with a knife. Bread was served by the oldest person present or by the host/hostess. Everyone took care that bread was never dropped directly onto the floor. If by an unlucky chance it was dropped, it was picked up, kissed and pressed to the forehead three times just as the Quran was when it was picked up. Only the right hand was used in eating; the left being used for unclean purposes such as washing the genital area. Concepts of food, impurity, and genital uncleanness were symbolically related. I was told that a married person who does not remove the pubic hair makes his food/bread unclean. The hair must be removed before it reaches the length of a grain of wheat.

Basic to any meal was bread baked in flat rounds. It was leavened with sour dough held from the previous baking. Tea was the most common drink. Schuyler reported that green tea was the traditional Central Asian drink and black tea was not known until it was introduced by the Russians (1887, I:126). According to Bacon, (1966:68) green tea was the most popular among Soviet Uzbeks; Shaniiazov notes that green tea was drunk in most of Uzbekistan with the exception of the Tashkent region (1974:52). Chagatay and Sjoberg also note the preference for black tea among the Tashkent *muhajirin* of Kabul (1955:77). Probably the entire Ferghana Valley region followed the Tashkent pattern and preferred black tea. It may be that under the Governate-General of Russian Turkestan, black tea was more available in those regions than in other parts of Uzbekistan. My informants generally preferred black tea; they explained that black tea was drunk to the regions north and east of the Afghan town of Pul-i Khumri and in Tajikistan, while green tea was drunk north and west of Pul-i Khumri and throughout most of Uzbekistan. However, at least one member of a *muhajir* family often preferred green tea over black. For that reason both kinds were always served at celebrations. Green tea was more often drunk in summer as it was believed to be cooling; black tea was classed as a warming food.

Of the two rice dishes most frequently served, *pilaw* was used in festive meals while *shulla* (Persian), *shawla* (Uzbek) which usually contained no meat, was the ordinary family meal. Basic *pilaw* was made with mutton, onions, rice, and carrots, but chicken, beef, horsemeat, raisins, and chickpeas also were used. *Shulla* was made with rice, oil, and pieces of carrots and potatoes. The Uzbek word, *ash*, that referred to these rice dishes took on the additional connotations of food and meal. The Uzbek word for kitchen thus was *ashkhana*, and the babytalk word for eat, hungry, feed me, as used by a one or two-year old was simply the repetition of *ash, ash*, whereupon the mother scooped up rice in her fingers and pressed it into the child's mouth. Yogurt was often added to soups and stews for flavor.

In the home, women prepared meals, dividing up the tasks so that perhaps one baked bread and another prepared rice. For community feasts and other large gatherings, men did the cooking of the *pilaw* in the mosque courtyard. *Pilaw* was brought back to the families after these gatherings. The rendered fat from the tail of the fat-tailed sheep was used in cooking for celebrations and was held to give a better flavor to *pilaw*. For daily use, various imported vegetable oils were used. One older informant said that people were becoming weaker as a result of eating only vegetable oil. She said that formerly when more animal fat was used, more boy babies were born, and now that vegetable oil was used, only girl babies were produced.

For entertainment of guests, the *distarkhan*, literally, tablecloth, was laid out. Tea, candies, bread, and seasonal delicacies were placed in front of each guest. It was considered proper that a guest stay for at least one meal and that some kind of meat dish be served. When especially important guests arrived, they were entertained at a different house for each meal until they left. The most honored visitors in the homes of the Kunduz Ferghanachis were the few relatives that managed to obtain permission in the Soviet Union to visit Afghanistan. An elderly Namangani woman escorted by one of her sons came to stay in her brother's house. This woman and her son were entertained, always in separate celebrations, for over three weeks. At least twenty other guests accompanied each of them to the various host households. These occasions offered the hosts the opportunity to compete with each other as to the quality and variety of foods set out. In one location, this woman was given the precious *aw-i zum zum*, water from the well near the Kaabah in Mecca.

Along with *pilaw*, guests were served *korma*, a side dish of seasonal vegetables such as spinach or cauliflower, or a meat and potato stew. A small amount of *korma* was picked up in the fingers and placed on the *pilaw* directly in front of the diner who then scooped up *korma* and *pilaw* together. Fresh vegetables, chopped tomato and onion, or cucumber were also served as a side dish. A favorite snack vegetable was *tarra*, a member of the cucumber family with light green fluted edges but longer than the familiar cucumber. Fresh fruits including apricots, mulberries, peaches, pears, apples, pomegranates, grapes, citrus fruits, and melons were also important to the diet.

Underlining the importance of melon in the diet was the fact that methods of its preparation and serving followed exact rules, each with a name. Schuyler first commented on this and provided an explanation which compared melon to meat:

> According to the Koran, when an animal is killed for food its throat must be cut in order that the blood may all run out. By transfer of ideas the melon is treated in the same way. First its throat is cut, that is, a small incision is made in the end farthest from the stem; then its head is cut off by slicing off a small piece; after that it is cut up lengthwise and with one or two dexterous turns of the knife the flesh is removed from the rind (1877, II:29).

While they began to cut each melon as described by Schuyler, my informants used a more complex system of preparation. When the rind was used as a dish, a watermelon was cut into two or four slices per section of rind, and a musk-melon was cut into three slices per section of rind. This was called *kasa* or bowl. When each slice of melon was cut into lengths the width of one bite, it was referred to as *qash* (Persian) or *telim* (Uzbek). When the melon was first cut into lengths and each length was divided into pieces, this was termed *kach*. Again, attention to detail, the ritual of food preparation, and rules of proper eating were emphasized.

The varieties of foods eaten, combinations of cooked foods, cooking methods, and the entire set of beliefs and customs regarding eating form one of the most stable complexes in Ferghanachi culture. There was little difference between my observations in this area and the account by Chagatay and Sjoberg forty years ago, Andreev's observation in Kasan in the 1920s or for that matter, Schuyler's descriptions one hundred years ago. There was also nearly complete continuity between various recipes in use by the Ferghanachi and descriptions of dishes still prepared in Uzbekistan described by Shaniiazov (1974). As might be expected, the Ferghanachi used the more traditional methods since they lacked electric or gas stoves, modern bakeries, and western-style cafeterias.

Food was a good ethnic indicator. The rounded Uzbek bread differed from bread made in other parts of Afghanistan. Certain foods such as *mantu*, a steamed dough filled with chopped meat, were known to be made in the North. More subtle differences were apparent between foods prepared by the Ferghanachi and other Uzbeks. *Halwa*, a pudding made of wheat, and *qatlama*, a fried pastry, were made by all Uzbek groups, but the methods of preparation differed as did the results. At weddings and other large celebrations where women from various groups brought home-made foods to share, anyone could easily tell the kind of ethnic background the maker of a particular food had. People generally felt the foods made according to their own ethnic prescriptions were superior. There was a good deal of whispered criticism of food preparation and presentation at any large gathering of women.

### The Household, the Kin Network and the Ethnic Group

The primary units of Ferghanachi social organization were the household, the kin network (kindred), and the ethnic group. The household was integrated though family ties based on economic productivity, social solidarity, and affective bonds. The division of labor within the household was based on distinctions of gender and age. Although the sexual division of labor was rigidly defined, within the household away from outsiders' eyes, some families made adjustments peculiar to their own domestic situation. For example, if there was only one woman within the household, and more than one adult man plus children who had to be fed, the woman's husband helped with so-called women's work, food preparation or cooking. I even saw a newly married man finish machine sewing a fringe on a scarf for his wife. At the time, he said to me that he had learned to sew from his mother. Certainly, in the bazaar all the tailors were men, so the skill was not confined to women. Still, the preparation of clothing for household use was defined as a female task.

When I questioned men about their doing so-called women's work, they were embarrassed, admitted that if their friends had seen them, they would have been ridiculed or pitied for having to help with such tasks. However, they either felt it was necessary for the sake of household harmony or that helping in an especially hectic time was worthwhile in itself. Women viewed help by men as unusual expressions of affection. Once, when a neighborwoman saw the remains of a meal cooked by a husband, she said to the wife, "He must really care about you." Elderly men were generally immune from sharing in the household chores. But it was often a grandfather who, desiring a special treat for himself, purchased meat, chicken, or *barra*, karakul lamb killed at birth, for a broth, and ended up cooking the broth and feeding the children.

Childcare was primarily the mother's, elder sister's, and grandmother's responsibility, though the father and uncles took on increasing authority for male children as they grew up. Boys were taken to the bazaar or to celebrations by household men. Even grandfathers picked up and amused babies when they cried if no one else was present. On one occasion in our household all the young men were out of town on business, so the household was made up of women and children plus the old patriarch whose own wife was with relatives in Saudi Arabia. The household was in an uproar because the baby was sick. The grandfather felt so responsible for the child and his son's family that he felt he should sleep in the same room with them at night. Then the baby cried all night, and the old man gave up his quest and retired on succeeding nights to the tranquility of the guesthouse.

It was much rarer for women to take on men's household tasks than it was for men to help women with theirs. The physical labor involved might have been a factor. In the one case I knew in which a woman did strenuous labor, piling poplar poles, and constructing a roof on her house, both she and others felt it was somehow unnatural. There was blame and bitterness expressed against this widow's two unmarried sons for not performing their household duties, thereby forcing their mother to do the work.

Operation of the household as an economic unit often included income contributed by both men and women. One example of a monthly family budget included: income from the retired father working parttime for the Spinzar company 900 afghanis; income from two adult sons 4350 afghanis; income from rental property 600 afghanis; income by adult women from embroidery sales, dairy product sales, and silkworm production 1000 afghanis. The total income per year averaged approximately sixty thousand afghanis. The income was high for Afghanistan (see Smith et al 1973:316-19), yet not particularly unusual for the Ferghanachis. The income earned by women was kept by them for household and their own expenses. At one time, the women in this household prepared dairy products from five cows. However, women's income obviously fluctuated a great deal from month to month. Some years silkworms were not raised; embroidered products were done on commission for other women, not for bazaar sale.

Food expenses in a monthly household budget for seven adults and four children included: five *ser* of rice at 600 afghanis; 12 *ser* of flour for 720 afs; six *ser* of potatoes at 190 afs; two *ser* of onions at 40 afs; three *ser* of carrots at 40 afs; other vegetables at 200 afs; 15-20 *ser* of cooking oil at 900 afs; meat at approximate 400 afs; tea at 150 afs; sugar, jam, candy at 200 afs for a total of 3450 afs. Other monthly expenses included electricity 250 afs, clothing 550 afs, livestock feed 300 afs, household items (soap, kerosene, etc.) 200 afs totalling 1300 afs. Seasonal expenses included: wood or other fuel 150 afs, transportation 1500 afs yearly, household repair 2000 afs yearly. A family also saved money for additional expenses if someone was sick, if there might be a marriage, or another celebration was anticipated. Celebrations frequently cost a family between 30-70,000 afghanis per year.

The Ferghanachis did not invest in land except for their *mahallas* and shops; all capital either was used in business, to purchase consumer items for the household which could later be sold, or to make the pilgrimage to Mecca, provide for ritual celebrations, etc. As a group, they fell into the urban middle classes in Afghanistan. For the most part without ties to the government, they were not part of the elite nor were they included in the poorest classes, landless laborers, or seasonal agricultural workers.

The household head was nominally the eldest male in the household, father or eldest brother, though a widow might be the head in the event her sons were young and had not yet married. Though the household head was always deferred to and treated respectfully, his role as economic provider was gradually usurped by sons. Tensions between fathers and sons often led to household fission. In fact, it was unusual for every son after marriage to remain in the father's household. However, at least one son and his wife always stayed.

Among the Kasani households in Kunduz, most included the three generational family with senior married couple, or surviving partner, and one or more sons with their spouses and children. Other Kasani households contained nuclear families; these included families whose oldest married children were daughters who lived elsewhere leaving a conjugal pair and younger children, and families with children just reaching marriageable age. Thus, household composition reflected the fact that virilocal residence was the norm and that married pairs usually determined the residence of their unmarried children within the context of their own virilocality.

Three generational households typical for the Ferghanachi are not necessarily to be considered a type of extended or joint family household in the classical anthropological sense. In the case of three generational families with dependent fathers or mothers attached to married couples, three generational households function as single nuclear families.

To constitute joint families, structurally and functionally, three generational households must include at least two nuclear families sharing economic and domestic responsibilities. In nuclear family households with dependent fathers or mothers, the son is the sole provider. Fathers and mothers do not discipline their grandchildren; they take care of them. To discipline is to have authority, to take care of is to receive instructions. Wives in these households, compared to mothers, command more influence than they do in functional joint family households, where mothers tend to dominate sons' wives (Khuri 1976:17).

The case of the Ferghanachi was perhaps midway between Khuri's example of Beirut in which three generational households function as nuclear families, and the traditional anthropological case in which three generational households function as joint families. The reason for this midway position lay in the differing roles each gender took on with age. Though men gained community respect when they achieved the status of elders in their sixties, it was also true that by this time they had often lost their role as economic providers. The role of economic provider carried household power, and the power of sons increased as that of their father waned.

The weakening position of the father was especially remarkable when contrasted with the increasing power of the mother. Not only did women gain respect as they aged, they also gained authority which they were able to retain. One partial explanation was the age difference between husbands and wives in the immigrant generation which provided a striking visual image: a woman in her fifties exercising authority in the household over her sons and daughters-in-law; her husband nearing seventy no longer running his bazaar shop, poring over the Quran in the *qarikhana* or a household room.

Unlike Khuri's nuclear family households in which there were either fathers or mothers dependent on the second generation couple, the Ferghanachi mothers were not dependent. In the conflicts between mother-in-law and daughter-in-law, mother-in-law was usually victorious. The position of father was more problematic; the loss of the economic role reverberated within the household and led to decreased authority which was glossed over by symbolic respect forms. The Ferghanachis insisted that religious knowledge was the ultimate source of authority and that men did not lose decision-making power within the household, but changing economic roles within the family obviously challenged the father's position.

Beside the conflicts between fathers and sons, the classic family conflict mentioned by informants was the incompatibility between mother-in-law and daughter-in-law. To a lesser extent, this conflict was echoed in the relations between a wife and her husband's unmarried sister or between daughters-in-law. Essentially, the various household tasks versus the pleasurable activities of visiting and shopping provided excuses through which a power struggle for household control and independent decision-making was conducted (Shalinsky 1989b).

The power hierarchy within the household, in theory, was understood to be a senior generation woman, then first daughter-in-law, second daughter-in-law, etc. following the order in which the sons took wives, equivalent to birth order. Unmarried daughters were supposed to be at the end. But in practice, mothers-in-law lent power to their own daughters at the expense of their sons' wives. Also, a second daughter-in-law was favored over a first if her kin connection to the mother-in-law was nearer. Subtle shifts in power relations in a household occurred over time.

Another potential source of family tension concerned the rearing of children. Again in theory, a man's brothers had authority over his children in his absence. Their decisions sometimes conflicted with the decisions of the children's mother. Corporal punishment including the use of switches was accepted for severe disobedience and mischief, but arguments often occurred about which person was to administer punishment and the degree to which the child was to be punished. Again, a hierarchy of power was worked out; a woman could successfully gain power over her husband's brothers if they were a good deal younger than she. However, the brothers might attempt to exercise what they viewed as their authority without consulting the woman at all. Both sides in family conflicts generally sought support from other household members.

The Quran permits a man to have up to four wives at a time if he treats them equally. However, polygyny was not common among the Ferghanachis: only ten to fifteen percent of the households involved polygynous marriage. Ferghanachi women pitied those involved in such marriages, mentioning acrimony and jealousy in a divided household. Apparently, most men preferred to spend money for consumer items and business improvements than for extra wives by the 1970s. Polygynous households functioned according to the same household composition rules as did monogamous households. Within the polygynous household, each wife maintained a separate home, furnishings, and supplies. Her own children resided with her.

Extreme formality characterized the relationship between co-wives. In one example, co-wives avoided visiting the same households simultaneously. On one occasion, they each visited a different neighbor and conducted a long distance fight, communicating via their children about who would return home. When one entertained guests, the guest saw only the wife who invited her and sat in her house. The guest properly was expected to greet and say goodby to the other wife by making the effort to visit her in the other house. The first wife never accompanied her to the other. Throughout the period of my stay in this neighborhood, the two women were present at the same woman's celebration only twice.

Despite the discord of a household with plural wives, men defended the practice on humanitarian grounds, the sickness of a first wife who should not be divorced, or a greatly loved first wife who is barren. Though these were ideal reasons given for polygyny, the economic condition of a man, that he could afford the expense, and his own inclination and desire because of a reputed beauty, were often the actual factors involved. Polygyny may have been slightly more common during the founding period of the *mahalla*. In one case, a man had a wife he left behind in Uzbekistan; he remarried in Afghanistan. Some years later he died but his wife showed me a photo album of her co-wife's family in Uzbekistan.

Despite the potential for conflict among household members, the household provided the most affectionate emotional bonds between people. Even women engaged in the struggle for control of the household developed a very intimate relationship. Common experience and help in childbirth or daily food preparation, mediation in marital arguments, joking, and even snowball fights bonded sisters-in-law. The household was a protected space whose reputation in the community depended on the cooperation and solidarity of all its members.

## Kin Network and Ethnic Community

Besides the household, most informants felt their obligations to kin were the most important despite the fact that the network of related households stretched beyond the immediate neighborhood to other towns in northern Afghanistan and Kabul. In times of crisis when support was needed, it was the kin network (kindred) which provided assistance. Generally, when social activities of the kin network and ethnic community conflicted, a rare occurrence, a household chose to maintain its strong connection to the kin network. The kin network was chosen even though daily social contact within the ethnic community, all the Ferghanachi households within a *mahalla*, was likely to be more frequent than contact with kin from other towns.

*Mahalla* Kasani contained approximately sixty households, a number which precluded daily contact between every household. Ideally, members from each household, no matter the ethnic group, were supposed to aid each other in life-crisis situations and join in celebrating religious festivals. In practice, this never occurred. Daily contact flowed along two pathways in the *mahalla*, the *kocha* (lane) pathway which linked three or four adjoining households, and the ethnic pathway which overlapped and included adjoining households, but overlooked geographical proximity. Each Ferghanachi household maintained most frequent contact with seven to ten of its geographically nearest fellow ethnic households. Because of the manner in which the *mahalla* was established, most of the Kasani households adjoined the common canal, but were not on the same *kocha*. Members from these households formed several basic social interaction units. Daily visits, frequent small gatherings, trips to the country or Kabul were visible signs of these interaction sets.

The neighbor relationship based on common *kocha* residence, was complicated by the multi-ethnic condition of the *mahalla*. Good neighbors were obligated to help each other with daily tasks as much as possible. Women were supposed to be free to drop in at a neighbor's to borrow a food item certain that it would be lent. Men were expected to utilize their skills for their neighbors as well as their own households. In practice, the expected *hamsaya* (Persian--neighbor) behavior developed only over a long period of time if the neighbors were not fellow ethnics. In fact, these relations often never developed except to the extent that non-Ferghanachi neighbors were invited to large celebrations such as weddings. The neighbor relationship did not develop between Ferghanachi and Pashtuns in the *mahalla*, though the relationship between Ferghanachis and Tajiks was more cordial. Nor did the neighbor relationship develop between any of the long-term residents and short-term renters.

Despite the patterns of neighborhood association which in some cases partially breached ethnic boundaries, social interaction within the *mahalla* was based primarily on ethnicity. Each Ferghanachi household's most frequent daily contacts when calculated over time were with the spatially nearest Ferghanachi households. A kinship relation between two such households increased the frequency of contact even more. Of the thirty-four *muhajir* households in *mahalla* Kasani, social interaction subsets were based upon town of origin in the *watan*, homeland. The fifteen Kasani households grouped themselves into several interaction subsets. The other *muhajir* Tajik households formed another subset. The Namangani households were also grouped into several micro-local interaction subsets. Obviously, these patterns of social relations developed over time because the Kasanis, who established the mahalla, built their compounds near each other as did the other *muhajir* groups who bought their land in the *mahalla* from the Kasanis. Thus, location within the *mahalla* and town origin tended to coincide.

The concept vital to the analysis of these patterns of social relations is *qawm*. Canfield (1973:34-35) defines *qawm* as a "locally conceived structural category" which is adjusted by the people involved to suit a particular social context. Canfield writes that

. . . the word *qawm* may be used to include not only those persons reckoning themselves agnates through a common ancestor, but also the persons who mutually assist each other and share goods with each other, not all of whom are always close kinsmen. It may apply to affinal as well as agnatic kinsmen, and even to unrelated persons who become assimilated into a group by marriage. And it may refer to friendly families who may eventually form kinship ties through reciprocal marriages. Conversely, the word can be contracted so as to exclude certain actual kinsmen who no longer cooperate with the rest of one's in-group.

The several ways in which the term *qawm* could be manipulated were particularly revealing in the case of the Ferghanachis. Because of the disruptive effects of the emigration, there were no agnatic descent group links people used to symbolically affirm their social bonding. They, therefore, replaced the notion of agnatic descent with common town origin. The small set of families that traced their origin to the same town in Uzbekistan was thus the smallest group calling themselves a *qawm*. But the people also wanted to demonstrate the endogamous nature of their groupings. The town origin sets were not large enough to be completely endogamous though that was the ideal. In solving the problem, the Ferghanachis came to accept the idea that a family which traced its origin to any Ferghana town could form part of the marriage pool. This collectivity known as "muhajirs" was also termed a *qawm*.

On the socio-linguistic level then, some people said that their qawm was Kasani or Namangani, while some said it was *muhajirin*.[1] Since the definitions of *qawm* used by Ferghanachi informants were historical rather than genealogical and geographical, in-group ethnically-based social relations necessarily transcended the *mahalla*. However, it was within the *mahalla* that proper *qawm* behavior was shown in daily visiting, reciprocity, ritual food sharing, and mutual aid.[2]

The kin network or kindred was composed of consanguineal and affinal links. From the perspective of an individual it began with those called by kin terms and faded with those others who were referred to as *khesh*, relatives. From a sociological perspective, the kin network linked families through different types of kin relations which theoretically could be extended until they coincided with *qawm* boundaries. Kin links to outsiders were possible but very rare. At the sociological limit, the *qawm* and the complex kin network were to a large extent interchangeable. Indeed, in the case of the Ferghanachis, social patterns of behavior between fellow *qawm* members and between members of a portion of a kin network functioned in the same manner. Mutual cooperation, attendance at life-crisis celebrations, financial assistance, and ritualized reciprocity characterized the social relations of each. The difference between the behavior of fellow *qawm* members and behavior within a kin network unit occurred only at the individual level. Thus, a man needing to borrow money for the pilgrimage to Mecca turned to his kin network and a portion of his *qawm*, his town origin group. He expected his kin to be more generous in their help than his *qawm*. Reciprocally, the obligation to help one's kin was stronger than the obligation to help *qawm*.

Marriage expanded the kin network of the spouses who were then combined into a conjugal unit, the wife retaining her natal network and gaining her husband's, the husband retaining his natal network and gaining his wife's. In addition, the rest of the household, as a unit, took on a new set of kin relations with the marriage of one of its members.

The test of the relative importance of natal network versus marital kin network once occurred when the two came into conflict. A woman had to fulfill both sets of obligations in a whirlwind of activity. She had prepared to attend a festive engagement celebration, *Shirin Khori*. A boy's female relatives (including the woman) were to deliver the trunks of bride clothes and display them to his fiance's female relatives and guests. As she prepared to leave, guests of her natal network, mother's sister's daughters, arrived for a visit. Since these women had come into the household, the obligations of hospitality demanded that they be given a spread of tea and sweets. This was prepared, tea was drunk, news was discussed. Then she accompanied her guests to another household in the neighborhood they wanted to visit. As it had grown late, she settled in at that household to drink tea when a message came for her to leave immediately. It seemed that the celebrants at the engagement party were so concerned that they sent a male relative with a truck to pick her up and take her to the party. As she had anticipated, by the time she arrived, she had time to complete the ritual greetings to everyone just as all the other guests were leaving. After staying about ten minutes, she also left. During our stay she had to explain the delay. When the woman explained that her own relatives had visited, the response was a brief nod and acceptance.

The woman's husband, however, was angry, because he felt that once his wife had escorted the guests outside the household compound, obligations to them were ended, and she should have left for the celebration. Since his mother and brother's wife were in Saudi Arabia, he felt that his wife stood in the place of his mother as the representative of the household. To absent the household from involvement in the celebration, even with the excuse of hospitality and lateness, was improper behavior in his view.

Allegiance and support within the kin network were most evident when circumstances confronted people with an emergency involving an outside agency. The decision-making group forced into quick action was frequently a segment of a kin network.

One day, an informant and I went to Khanabad. We were driven back toward evening by the informant's mother's brother's daughter's son who, unknown to me, had no driver's license though he owned a Toyota truck. Midway between Khanabad and Kunduz, as we drove, we could see a ten-year old boy playing in the middle of the highway. The boy threw a hat in the path of our on-coming car. Though the driver tried to swerve, he was helpless, and the truck ran over the boy. Everyone knew he was killed instantly. Unfortunately, because of the impact, the control of the car was in jeopardy. First we swerved to the left, and then to avoid a post, to the right, where the truck turned over on its side. The police were immediately on the scene since they were only two cars in front of the truck on the road.

I later found out that a driver without a license who kills a person was always considered at fault, and the minimum prison sentence was ten years. For a licensed driver, the minimum sentence was only two years in prison. These circumstances set up an immediate crisis for the kin network. The man involved was the chief economic provider for his household. He was married with children. After dropping me in Kunduz, my informant returned to Khanabad for three days to participate in the decisions and actions of his kin network. As it turned out, injury to a man on the truck was not as bad as feared. The basic dilemma facing the network was bribery of the police and the subsequent substitution of another man with a license for the driver. By the night of the accident, the driver had been freed from the police and had temporarily gone into hiding in Kabul. Meanwhile, his male kin were attempting to raise the needed additional funds and to decide on a substitute. Luckily, among the male kin was a young man with a license and without a family who, with the network's compensation, agreed to go before the judge saying that he was the driver. The family that lost the son was also compensated. The potentially nasty situation was neutralized by the quick action of the kin network. As evidence concerning the speed in which a network can be mobilized, I later met other members of the network which stretched from Khanabad to Kabul who told me they had heard of the accident the day after its occurrence. The news of my minor injury in the accident was soon known throughout the Ferghanachi community as apparent in the solicitous remarks people made when seeing me at various celebrations thereafter. I was supposed to inform the provincial governor whenever I left Kunduz; however, the police and the government never found out my involvement, demonstrating the strong secrecy boundary at the *qawm* level.

As discussed previously, frequent contact between families had a neighborhood and ethnic basis emphasizing the horizontal links between families. Casson (1974:347-73) in his analysis of social structure in a central Anatolian village described a similar social organization. The principal unit of social structure in that village was the household rather than the patrilineal descent group. Bilaterality was the fundamental rule of kin relations even though the men's and women's communities functioned separately. In other words, one maintained kin relations with those persons linked to ego through father, mother, and spouse. Yet women saw only the female half of these relatives and men saw only the male half.

Related to the issue of bilaterality were Ferghanachi marriage preferences. Traditional ethnographies of the Middle East often state that people prefer that a young man marry his father's brother's daughter, the closest eligible girl based on patrilineal relationship. While Ferghanachis were familiar with this idea, many generalized it to include either parent's sibling's child. In fact, the preference would be more appropriately stated as marriage with someone to whom kin links were traceable. The horizontal connections between households linked through marriage provided the fundamental structuring factor of Ferghanachi social organization. The principle of bilaterality was expressed in kinship terms and social relations within the kin network.

## NOTES

1. For *qawm*, some occasionally said Uzbek although this was more often a reponse to a broader question about peoplehood using the Persian word, *mardom*.

2. The Ferghanachis used the word, *qawm*, in both Persian and Uzbek. Other Uzbek groups apparently have other terms which may incorporate a more strict notion of agnatic descent (Zhilina 1974:60).

# Chapter 5

# Gender

Within the Ferghanachi household and in their Kunduz neighborhoods, gender was the characteristic that most determined the changing roles that people played as they moved through the life cycle. Gender includes the social constructions and conventions that overlie the biological differences between the sexes. Societies often use life cycle rituals to enforce appropriate gender roles. For the Ferghanachis, the birth of a child had significance not only for the new life, but also for the woman, a newly created mother, and other adults associated with the event. A wedding involved not only bride and groom, but transformed the household and the relations between households. Birth and childhood, marriage, adulthood, old age, and death were marked with rituals of transition which guided individuals as they confronted their own changing identities and the identities of others.

Ferghanachi women rarely went to Spinzar hospital for childbirth though pain-killing shots administered by travelling nurses from the family services clinic were sometimes used along with the traditional midwife or mother-in-law to attend the birth. The new child was named three days after birth by some method based on family discussion. Often the Quran was opened and the first appropriate name on the page was given to the child. The first celebration for the baby, a women's gathering, occurred the sixth night after the birth. Before that time, close women relatives or friends brought gifts of food for the mother.

About forty days after birth, the child was bound into a cradle for the first time. He/she spent sleeping time until the age of one to two years bound in the cradle. A women's celebration known as *beshik tuy* (Uzbek) or *gahwara tuy* (Persian) was sometimes held in honor of the cradle binding. Only after forty days of childbirth seclusion (*chilla qashti*--Uzbek) did the mother leave her house. During this forty day period, she was thought dangerous to other pregnant women, who did not visit her. In addition to her potential to cause harm, the mother was uniquely vulnerable to evil at this time and had to be protected (Snesarev 1972, 10(3):271). Miscarriage was often attributed to the influence of a barren woman, a woman whose child had died, or a woman who left her home before forty days and crossed the path of the pregnant woman. Thus the *beshik tuy* served as a rite of passage for the baby and the mother, who emerged into the community of adult women and their children for the first time.

For the first few months of life, the child was swaddled and bound even outside the cradle. At six or seven months, the arms were allowed to remain free; gradually, the legs were also allowed to remain unbound at all times except at night when the child was again put into the cradle. At about ten months, the child was propped up so he/she could learn to sit upright, and placed on its stomach to learn to crawl. Mothers began to give small amounts of solid food during this time.

The breast was given decreasingly until it was given only at night after the child was bound in the cradle. Weaning from the cradle and the breast took place when the child was 1½ or 2 years old. To encourage the child to stop wanting to nurse, the mother pricked her child with a needle, or put foul-tasting medicine on her nipple.

When a baby was born, regardless of sex, his parents kept track of the year; perhaps the mother would remember the season, but soon a child learned to count the names of the years in a cycle which repeated every thirteen years: mouse, cow, tiger, rabbit, fish, snake, horse, sheep, monkey, chicken, dog, pig. As Schuyler noted (1877, I:333) everyone born the same year was considered the same age. There were several interesting folk beliefs connected to these animal years. The animals were classified into *haram*, the animals which cannot be eaten; and *hallal*, the animals which can be eaten. When a person who was born in the year of *haram* animal twitched his left eyelid inadvertently, he was believed to have good luck. If it was his right eyelid, he was thought to have bad luck. For a person born in a year of a *hallal* animal, right eyelid twitching was good and left eyelid popping was bad.

Even at pre-toddler age, adults imposed rules of proper conduct. Until the circumcision celebration (*sunnat tuy*), held at age 3 or 4,[1] the little boy was allowed to roam freely without trousers through the household yard and in front of guests. He learned to squat down anywhere in the yard to urinate and defecate and an adult cleaned the yard. Women fondled his penis and teased him about its size and being a man. After circumcision, the boy was expected to behave more modestly, leave his trousers on, and use the bathroom shed. At age six, most boys began attending both public and religious school.

From the beginning, different standards of modesty were in effect for the little girl. The few times that mothers attempted to leave their girl children's genital region uncovered because of the heat, their husbands objected strongly. Girls at any age must not be *bi-sharm*, immodest. Even when girls played with their friends, they frequently had a little brother or sister in their arms. Generally, they were considered more responsible at a younger age than boys. Girls and boys usually played separately although related children sometimes played together. Girls also attended public school, perhaps until sixth class. They attended religious classes with a woman learned in the Quran called *bibi-mullah* (Persian), or *atin aya* (Uzbek). Boys attended the *bibi-mullah's* class until they were able to read the Arabic alphabet and knew a few prayers. Then they attended the *qarikhana*

*Photo 5.1 Baby bound into cradle.*

*Photo 5.2
Ferghanachi
mother
and
child*

(study house of the mosque) to learn proper recitation and memorization of the Quran. At the *bibi-mullah's*, girls also learned to read the Quran. Until the 1960s, this was often the only formal education girls were allowed.

High schools in Afghanistan generally were segregated according to sex. Despite this separation, some Ferghanachi girls left school at the age of puberty, when they adopted the veil. For the first time in *mahalla* Kasani, a local Ferghanachi girl completed the twelfth class of high school in 1977. She and other school girls wore the veil at night when attending celebrations, when visiting the bazaar, and when visiting neighbors' homes where strangers or older men were present. But to and from school, they wore the school uniform. Public education for girls and the delay of the adoption of the veil created controversy and heated family discussion about the propriety of these acts as they related to the marriage potential of daughters. It was not necessarily the mother who supported her daughter's aspirations for education nor was it the father who opposed. Women played an extremely important role in the arrangement of marriages, and women's gossip about a girl's behavior could be very damaging. In the case of the Kasani girl who completed high school, her mother had fought against her attendance, but her father had permitted her to go even though a good deal of community sentiment was against it. This girl was not allowed to attend Kabul University though she passed the entrance exam with a high score. Some boys from the *mahalla* did attend university beginning during the 1960s. Many boys completed high school while they spent increased time working in their father's or a relative's shop. They were usually well-established in the bazaar by the time they reached marriageable age.

## Marriage

Traditionally, for a girl the veil indicated not only puberty, but also marriageability; the latter followed quickly after the former. The first set of Ferghanachi marriages in Afghanistan during the 1930s and 1940s involved women from twelve to fourteen years of age. Gradually, the age considered most suitable for marriage increased. By the 1970s, a good marriageable age was thought to be from seventeen to twenty-one for girls and from twenty to twenty-five for boys.

The parents of a boy decided when he was ready for marriage; they must have had or been able to borrow enough disposable assets to allow for their payment of bridewealth and the celebrations they must host. All the families in the *qawm,* ethnic group, who had eligible daughters were discussed, but usually the boy's mother had in mind several suitable girls whom she thought would best fit the household situation. Informants, particularly married women, felt that too close a relative for a spouse led to marital disharmony, because the individuals involved would have known each other as childhood playmates and would have been accustomed to arguing with each other. These women felt that marriages between second or third degree collaterals offered the best chance for a good marriage.

A boy's mother discussed a few possible matches with her son, but she generally had in mind the girl she favored. She then sent a neighborwoman or relative to sound out the girl's mother on the subject of a proposed match. If the response to this initial inquiry was favorable, she and a group of her friends visited the girl's mother themselves. The boy's mother and friends visited the girl's house several times, while the girl's mother consulted her husband, who in turn consulted his male relatives.

When the two fathers exchanged the *aqlik*, a sort of a white cloth,[2] the couple was officially betrothed. The *aqlik* served the same purpose as a contract; at this point neither party could back out of the agreement. Through intermediaries, discussion began concerning the amount of food the groom's family should provide for the wedding, and clothes and household goods required for the bridegift. The betrothal was officially announced at a men's celebration during which each guest was given a white handkerchief filled with candies. Later a women's celebration took place at the bride's mother's house. During this celebration the future groom's female relatives ritually presented the brideclothes and gifts, which were displayed to all the guests.

Only about two weeks before the actual wedding was the final agreement on the brideprice, a cash payment, reached. For the Kunduz Ferghanachis, this averaged in the five thousand to twenty thousand afghani range ($125-$500). Until the 1960s, brideprices were usually less than 10,000 afs, but the 1970s price had seen some inflation. Each girl also brought a dowry of clothes, bedding, household goods, and embroidered decorative items to her new home. The relatively low brideprice given to the girl's father, combined with the dowry that the girl's side provided, in practice meant that the girl's father and brothers did not obtain financial gain from the marriage. Apparently, the equivalence of dowry from the bride's side and brideprice from the groom's was a Central Asian oasis pattern (Bacon 1966:68-9). Husband-wife informants originally from Uzbek villages near Andkhoi told me that typical brideprice there ranged from 25,000 afs, and that the payment which was included in their own marriage settlement was 100,000 afs, since they were not related. The Andkhoi situation might have involved the high Turkmen brideprice pattern adopted by Uzbeks, but even so, the low Ferghanachi brideprice served as an ethnic characteristic and facilitated in-group marriage.

The day of the wedding was set according to auspicious days. Certain periods of the year such as the time immediately after Ramadan were considered appropriate for weddings. The length of the engagement varied from two weeks to as much as a year; in normal circumstances, the boy's side urged that the wedding be held as soon as possible while the girl's side sought to delay.

As the arrangements were finalized in the pre-nuptial period, a contest between the groom's side and the bride's side conducted by the women of each began. The contest was in some aspects a prestige game, but at its core were the conflicting loyalties which women felt were inherent to the girl/bride (Shalinsky 1984). She had been living in her natal household where, ideally, and indeed, based on my observations, she was protected and treated affectionately. Now she must give her loyalty and trust to members of another household where she must contribute to a working group of women.

The girl's side was allowed to express its feelings and control over the bride through two mechanisms, the recital of ritual wedding songs and the enforcement of suitable bride behavior. The most important wedding song sung by Ferghanachi women was *Yar Yar*, the Uzbek lovers' song. The song was sung whenever the bride was escorted out of her house to the yard, when she was escorted to meet the groom, when she was escorted to the groom's house, and finally at the *yuz achti* when the secluded bride in her new home was escorted out for the ritual unveiling before the community of women.

The *Yar Yar* song, known in many different versions with different words and tunes from Andkhoi to Ferghana, elicited many emotions; women often wept as it was sung. The version favored by the *muhajirs* contained so many verses that the singing often lasted nearly a half hour. While some verses dealt with the beauty of the bride and the clothes and jewels she was given, there were verses which described the supposedly forlorn bride. In one verse, she was likened to an orphan without a family given over to strangers. The tune was mournful. To the accompaniment of the *daira* drum, the procession of kin and friends on each side of the bride sang *Yar Yar*. Appropriate verses were chosen on the spur of the moment to reflect the tension, suppressed joy, and sadness of each wedding.

> I.My father has fired the black and white pistols/
> My father has sold his own daughter without realizing/
> Now that his daughter is gone, he should plant almonds/
> The shaking of the almond branches will recall his child.
> II.   Don't throw the stone in the river because it will not return/
> Don't give your daughter far away, he will take her and go/
> The one who gives her daughter far away has a pale face/
> Tears from her eyes flow like a stream/
> The tears are not like a [narrow] stream but like a lattice screen/
> The poor girl bears every kind of cruelty. (Shalinsky 1989a:135)

The bride's kinswomen also controlled the bride's behavior through lectures and admonition that she present a sad downcast face and reluctance to leave. They cautioned that to appear otherwise looked shameless before the new in-laws and the community. Many girls looked forward to marriage and were quite pleased to be the center of attention at their wedding celebrations; they enjoyed receiving new clothes and household items, and eagerly anticipated their new status as married women. These girls were cautioned by their relatives and friends that to show delight augured badly for the marriage and could bring the evil eye.

The messages conveyed by all the ritual activities during the celebrations before and after marriage was ambiguous. The bride's relatives and friends expressed happiness as well as grief. They danced to show pleasure at the good fortune of the bride. The happiness expressed at the celebration was aimed toward the future when the bride had her own children and the management of her own household while the sadness pointed to her current situation when she must learn to obey strangers.

If the actual marriage contract was to be signed on Friday, the evening before, Thursday night, was the *shaw-i khinna*, the night of the henna. Girls from among the groom's relatives, led by his sisters, went to a party at the bride's mother's. After eating and dancing, seven girls dabbed the bride's right hand with henna, the beginning of the beauty preparations the bride made before she saw her new husband for the first time and was escorted to her new home. The bride's left hand was also dyed, and usually the groom's relatives brought enough henna so that all the guests' hands were dyed.

Friday before the guests arrived while all the food was readied, a mosque official and witnesses visited the boy and later the girl to ask if they consented to the marriage. The marriage contract, *nikah*, was signed, and the marriage was officially sanctioned. The groom and his peers celebrated with jokes and dancing. In preparation for meeting his bride and escorting her home, the groom changed into a special *koinak* and *ishtan, chapan*, cap, and turban provided by the bride's family. Older men did not attend this party, but they were entertained at an afternoon celebration at the boy's house.

Meanwhile, at the bride's mother's house, the women from both sides gathered for a festive meal and dancing. Sometime after midnight, the women sent word to the boy that his bride was ready. He and only two or three of his closest friends then entered the women's celebration. As the groom was escorted into the yard in front of two hundred fifty or three hundred women, his bride was escorted from the house by her closest friends and relatives. She was supposed to maintain a downcast face at all times and often cried before departure as did her relatives. The bride and groom were both led in front of a decorated bench. Each tried to be the last to sit down. The groom's friends danced in front of the women, but they soon left. The couple was then entertained by the women's and girls' dancing. Some time in the early morning hours, all the women escorted the couple to the groom's household where a new room had been prepared. The wedding was announced to all corners of the town by carts of guests (in the 1970s hired buses and cars filled with women) who were driven to each side of town before arriving at the groom's house. At the groom's household, there was more singing and dancing. Finally, the groom's closest female relatives escorted the couple into their new room where they piled up twenty or more mattresses on the middle of the floor. The relatives placed the couple on the mattresses, piled on blankets, and retired to a curtained area (*chimiliq*--Uzbek) within the same room. The women occasionally made various comments concerning the groom's behavior. Sexual intercourse sometimes did not take place under such circumstances. Perhaps the presence of these women with the bridal couple cushioned the shock of sexual initiation for the bride.

On the day following the *nikah,* the groom's family received the bride's mother and relatives along with the most important women of the community. The celebration included a meal, a ritual enactment of the bride's new household duties, and a symbolic acceptance of her new status as a married woman by the other women in the community. These ritual events were called *yuz achti* (Uzbek= opening, unveiling the face). There is no exact equivalent term in Persian since the ceremony has no counterpart in non-Uzbek groups. The celebratory *takht jami* performed in Persian-speaking households involved only the viewing of the bride's new room and did not include the other rituals of the *yuz achti*. However, the *yuz achti* ceremony did have a unique Kasani term, indicating that it was a traditional part of the wedding ritual in Kasan. The Kasani term is *rukshan*, a shortened form of *ruy koshan*, similar to the Uzbek *yuz achti* in meaning as it also referred to uncovering the face.

When the guests arrived, the bride was secluded behind a curtain hung from the ceiling to the floor in her new room. She was greeted by the guests and her demeanor was carefully observed. She must be veiled and downcast. After the meal, gifts were presented to the groom's family by the bride's mother and relatives. Gifts for male relatives of the groom were also given including specially made *chapans* and turban cloths and caps. The bride was escorted to an area set up for ritual gift-giving. Each member of the women's community slowly took forward her gifts to the bride. The most frequently given gifts were thin scarves, which were placed on top of the bride's own veil. The giver then lifted the veil aside and kissed the bride. The giver stepped back, and the bride, helped by two relatives, one on each side, made three bows from the waist in acknowledgment. After the giftgiving, the veil was removed, and the bride was seated before a table with flour and cooking fat on it. The mother-in-law poured flour into the bride's hands which were cupped. After the flour, the mother-in-law filled the bride's hands with *roghan*, cooking fat, used in the preparation of the various rice dishes.

Finally, the bride's hands were filled with candy three times and she strewed the candy all around her while the women scrambled to get the lucky candy. At the conclusion of the ritual, the mother-in-law instructed the bride whom she was to acknowledge through her bowings. The recital brought tears to the eyes of the onlookers as the bride salaamed her husband's kin, everyone's friends in Saudi Arabia, Kabul, the Soviet Union, and everyone's dead ancestors. Weddings were essentially women's rituals. The marriage rite in many ways can be thought of as a ceremony of women joining other women and an enhancement of women's solidarity (Fallers 1976:254).

The night after the *yuz achti*, the second night of the marriage, the bride's sister stayed in a nearby room to keep her sister company and ensured that the new bride maintained a modest demeanor. The sister then removed the bedclothes to her own household the next morning as proof of virginity. For the next forty days, the bride was secluded, never leaving her new household compound. Each morning she made the requisite bowings to her in-laws. She was also supposed to bow when meeting her husband. Women continued to visit the bride in her new home, where all her new belongings were displayed on the walls for a week after the wedding.

A new bride traditionally did not leave her house before the birth of her first child. While it was still considered improper for a bride to visit her own family and friends frequently, strict seclusion was not enforced in the 1970s. Instead, a ceremony was introduced whereby the bride was received by her friends and kin who acknowledged her new status. The celebration was called *kilenchaqirdi* (Uzbek=bride welcoming). Usually several brides were honored at once. As the bride entered the hostess's interior door, candy and coins were strewn over her. The guests and children scrambled for the goodies as the bride entered and bowed from the waist. Each time the ritual greeting was completed for a newly arrived guest, the bride rose and bowed. As the special guest, she received extra gifts from the hostess.

Bride welcoming rituals were given throughout the year of marriage even after the bride had a child. The ritual simply indicated that the bride was visiting a particular household for the first time since her status had changed. Usually, some time in the second year of marriage, a bride had been "welcomed" by all the households to which she was tied via kinship or ethnic association. At this point, she became another married woman guest when visiting.

Progression in the female life cycle was tied to natural changes and the social consequences of those changes. The wearing of the veil, physical maturity including menstruation, and marriage traditionally were closely linked. Indeed, since loss of virginity, pregnancy, and childbirth were also linked to marriage, the girl faced a series of changes in a relatively short period of time. Though a girl learned some negative aspects of female gender identity which were associated with impurity, womanhood also included the positive endpoints, mother, house-hold manager, and equal member of women's society. Within the series of wedding rituals, the girl was led to deal with and minimize the negative aspects, which included relations with her husband, and to maximize the positive aspects, especially membership in the community of women.

For the boy, marriage did not articulate or resolve all the problems associated with manhood. The wedding ritual from the groom's point of view was unidirectional; he was introduced to his wife, to sexuality, and thereby to impurity. His experience thus differed from his bride's. The various rituals and celebrations that highlight the special position of a bride had no counterpart in the life of a man. As a groom, he continued the work pattern previously developed within his father's shop and his mother's household. When children came, he gained prestige and became more of a figure of authority in his own right, but a man's changing status as he aged was subject to a much more gradual process than the abrupt change marking a woman's transition from virgin daughter to wife and mother.

The men's community had almost no role to play in wedding festivities. A mosque official and witnesses visited the boy and the girl to ask if they consented to the marriage. The marriage contract, *nikah*, was signed and the marriage was official. All this activity took place before the celebration of *shaw-i nikah*. Older men, numbering perhaps one or two rooms full, were entertained at an afternoon celebration at the boy's house, but there was no celebration by the entire men's community. On *shaw-i nikah*, the night after the contract was signed, the boy usually had a small party of 10 to 30 men, with only his peers present. At this party, the boy changed into clothes including *chapan*, cap, and turban prepared by the bride's family. Significantly, informants said that the wedding party was often the first time a boy wore a turban. It seems, then, that the wedding did symbolize to some extent the achievement of manhood. The symbol of male adulthood was the religious symbol, the turban cloth, which the young man only began to consistently wear much later when he reached his thirties.

When the groom was called by his kinswomen into the women's celebration on *shaw-i nikah*, the ostensible reason was to escort his bride back to their new house. However, the groom suffered a test before he was allowed to accomplish his purpose. The groom entered the women's celebration with only two or three friends to support him. He faced two or three hundred women who were staring critically. This was the only time as an adult male that the groom saw the blur of faces of most of these women. The groom walked slowly, deliberately, and solemnly with face down. He forced himself to avoid the brink of nervous laughter which he squelched by a large white handkerchief held over his mouth. Thus, in a sense, both the groom and bride were veiled when they first faced each other. The entrance of the groom and the converging approach of the newly married pair were the high points of the night's activities for the female audience.

Some Ferghanachi grooms wore western-style dress to the celebration with the modern style karakul hat. They wished to present a sophisticated appearance for the women's approval. Some few fortified themselves with liquor to help them face the ordeal. Of course, the women were unaware of this fact and would have strongly disapproved. The long uncomfortable approach to the bride demonstrated to the groom that another world existed about which he had known nothing, that women were its guardians, and that he should rely on women if he wanted to learn its secrets. Surprisingly, the groom found that he could not be a man unless he learned about woman from women.

As mentioned previously, the bride and groom were put to bed by the groom's own female relatives. Some sat up all night within the room behind a curtain. Other women did not return to their own households, but stayed the night in other household rooms. The groom was thus surrounded by women, not to mention his own bride. Many boys were intimidated by this situation and were not able to initiate intercourse. For women to control a man through control of his sexual performance would be a good way to maintain power over him. It is a grave error to assume that women were without power when they controlled this fundamental aspect of a man's life.

The wedding ritual served a two-fold purpose. It operated as a group dynamic. Groom and bride were judged by the women's community, accepted, and formed into a new procreative unit. On the individual level, only the girl was directed toward the fulfillment of her "nature" and into the adult women's community. Thus women almost completely controlled marriage from its arrangements and rituals through its consequences.

### Gender Ideology

The life of adult women revolved around family. Childbearing and nurturing were important tasks. Bodily functions such as menstruation, sexual intercourse, and pregnancy were part of each woman's ordinary experience. Attitudes toward these reveal much about conceptions of gender.

The periodic menstrual "uncleanness" of women was generalized into an attitude about women as an entity apart. I was told that a woman who does not purify herself for forty days will become an *almasti* (*albasti* in many Uzbek dialects). *Almastis* have long dirty hair which they comb constantly and a bad smell. They sit in dark places, especially near the *juy* (canal) entrance in abandoned compound walls. Though not explicit, there was a definite connotation of female sexuality become evil and perverted as it was not regulated and purified. The *almasti* obviously failed to perform the necessary purification after at least one menstrual period.

Menstrual blood was viewed as ritually defiling. Women with their periods were excused from daily performance of prayers until after they had again become purified. Though defiled by menstrual blood, the *almasti* gained several powers including the ability to disappear and the ability to cause illness and insanity. *Almastis* were described as sitting on horses and frightening them, which also involved symbolic sexual power, possibly over men. One story known by many was that some people had formerly owned a horse with an exceptionally long mane. Every morning for a week, they woke up to find the mane of this horse braided. Everyone believed that this was done by an *almasti* (see also Snesarev 1971, 9(3):338).

In a way the *almasti* became a symbol of women who were beyond the control of men. I once attended a party at a neighborwoman's house, which was attended by several women teachers from the Kunduz girls' school. These women did not wear the veil. Returning from the evening prayers at the local mosque, Haji Omar got a clear view of these women as they left and entered the street. When we returned to our own household compound, Haji Omar said to me sarcastically, "Did you see all the almastis?" implying not only female immodesty, but also ugliness and improper womanhood (Shalinsky 1986: 332-334).

Interestingly, there was no discernible Islamic context that related to *almastis*. It was the only case in which a popular belief relating to a supernatural creature was linked neither to the Quran nor to any Islamic heroic figure. For the Ferghanachis, the creature provided a distorted image of womanhood. Associated with menstrual blood, the *almasti* also combined other "improper" sexual symbols. The long unclean hair may be a symbolic reference to the defiling unplucked pubic hair. A woman informant once said that "the unbelieving Hindus" let their pubic hair grow so long that they braid it, a comment which recalls the *almasti* who braided the horse's mane.

Ferghanachi women took care to perform the purification rituals correctly. They used pieces of cloth to catch the menstrual flow. These were then washed out with soap and water, and thus purified, they were re-used. In the bazaar of Kunduz, western-style women's sanitary products were available in a few of the largest stores. Most women did not know how these products were used, but they were aware that they were thrown away and not washed. I was informed that to throw blood away like that was a sinful practice.

Purification after menstruation took place either in the household washroom or in a public bath which had small private rooms. For reasons of modesty, it did not take place in the regular public bath communal rooms. Sexual intercourse during the menstrual period was prohibited.

First sexual intercourse after a wedding transformed the status of a girl to that of a woman. In both the Persian *dukhtar* and the Uzbek *qiz*, the word for daughter, girl, and virgin was a single lexical item. The notion of the virgin/daughter was associated with the protection from outsiders inside her father's household compound. After marriage, a woman had the same protection at her new home except that her husband and she had sexual intercourse. The only other operational category for women was prostitute. If for some reason, a woman was not a virgin and yet she was unmarried, she automatically was relegated to this category. A married woman with a lover was also placed in this category. The boundaries of the categorization were rigid. Once stigmatized as a prostitute, a woman had no recourse and could not again become a respectable married woman.

Some women readily admitted enjoying being with their husbands and some were embarrassed to talk about intercourse. The common forms of sexual foreplay were kissing and manipulation of a woman's breasts by the man. Women noted that men like to play with big breasts and some were quite proud of their figures.[3] When husbands and wives had intercourse, they did not remove their clothing but kissing and breast play took place over or under clothes. The trousers were lowered for intercourse. Intercourse took place at night. Most couples had a wooden bed frame with several piled mattresses for use during intercourse. For sleeping, a mattress was placed on the floor for each individual. Couples never spent the whole night together on the bed.

There were several ways to refer to sexual relations. The most common fairly polite euphemism was to call it "sleeping together in one place." In fact, it was commonly thought that any man and woman alone together would "sleep in one place." Other terms for sexual relations included the Persian *bazi* which can refer to dancing and games as well as sexual intercourse since it connotes "play." The Uzbek, *oynashmak*, to play together, was used similarly.

After intercourse, women performed the usual ablution at home. Men purified themselves at the public bath or in the nearby canal by complete immersion in water. Sexual intercourse was thus defined as an unclean act. Purification took place before the next daily prayer. Since the public baths opened at 4 a.m., men rose early and proceeded to the bathhouse before beginning the day's work.

In addition to their wives, men did have access to the professional prostitutes. Belonging to ethnic groups referred to as Loli or Jogi, encampments of prostitutes were found along well-travelled routes short distances from towns or villages. Decisions about sexual behavior made by men resulted from their feelings regarding religious sanctions, morality, and about their wives.

Many young married couples were concerned with maintaining a smaller family size than was common in the past. Where once eight to ten pregnancies per woman was the norm, couples wanted to limit their families to four or five children. The basic reason for the new desire appeared to be economic. The availability of consumer/luxury goods had increased the desire for the accumulation of capital. Perhaps the emphasis on money made children seem a less important investment in the future. Improving survival rates for children as health care improved were also a factor.[4] While older informants felt that God provided for the children he gave, new attitudes regarding contraception were most common among the secularly well-educated. Often men introduced these ideas to their wives.

In Kunduz, the family planning clinic made available all modern methods of contraception including the pill, IUDs, diaphragms, condoms, and contraceptive jelly. None of these methods had made much of an impact among the Ferghanachis. All were viewed as sinful, which prevented their utilization by some couples. The physical exam of women by male doctors precluded the use of some methods. The pill was used by a few couples in mahalla Kasani (non-*muhajirs*) but was considered dangerous by most women.[5] Condoms were also sold in the bazaar, but mostly to children who used them as balloons. Mothers, with some embarrassment, confiscated them from the children so, no doubt, their function was known to some. Withdrawal and abstinence provided the most commonly used contraceptive techniques. In addition, breast feeding for the first two years after the birth of a child possibly provided some contraceptive action during that period.

In the family services clinic in the waiting area where mothers took their babies for inoculations, there were diagrams of the female internal reproductive organs, pregnancy, and the means by which pregnancy was mechanically prevented. Most of the time the diagrams were ignored, but once a Ferghanachi woman did study the diagrams. She spoke only two statements regarding the diagrams, one a question as to whether a particular organ was the *tukhumdan*, the egg-producing organ of the woman, and the other statement that such shameful pictures should not be on display. The response of this woman to the diagrams indicates common attitudes about pregnancy. In addition to shame, there was a rather vague notion that the woman has seeds or eggs (the term for the two being the same) which work in the formation of the baby. This belief was well-illustrated in the joke-riddle, --How is a woman like a pumpkin? The answer was that both are filled with seeds.[6] Conception was understood to be the result of sexual intercourse.

Apart from conversation about miscarriage, mention of pregnancy was rare. Married women especially those pregnant with their first child hid their condition as long as possible. Other women usually spotted the signs of pregnancy and forced the pregnant woman to admit her condition through teasing. A woman who attempted abortion was thought evil. Knowledge of herbal concoctions used as abortifacients was apparently hidden or not wide-spread. Women reportedly obtained the mixtures from the Hindu herbal doctors. Despite the belief that women should conceive and bear children, the condition of pregnancy carried shame. Pregnancy was a visible reminder of the sexual union and as such was associated with similar attitudes and behavior.

Part of the gender ideology of the Ferghanachis was based upon the belief that a struggle between two inclinations takes place within people. *Nafs* (desire), including all types of personal indulgence such as lust and greed, wars with *aql* (reason), developed through studying the Quran which then is used by the individual to control *nafs*. *Fitna* is the chaos that can result in a society where *aql* remains undeveloped and *nafs* reigns unchecked. If *nafs* is controlled through the social mechanism of marriage, the Muslim community is strengthened through the procreation of children and *fitna* does not result (Shalinsky 1986).

Women were frequently equated with *nafs* and were often portrayed as sexually insatiable, because their innate passions overwhelmed their reason. As in most of the Middle East, the Ferghanachis believed a man and a woman left alone together will have sex, because the woman tempts and the man cannot resist. Popular Islamic texts in the mosque schools taught this. The Ferghanachi mosque in Kunduz used the Persian language Islamic text, *Kulliyati Chahar Kitab*, which included poetic passages that said that the desire to give up *nafs* is weak, the worship of God will weaken *nafs*, and the characteristics of the witless and ignorant are companionship with the immature and preoccupation with women and sex. Laziness, immodesty, propensity to anger, concern with self-adornment and lack of concern for domestic tasks were considered women's faults and the consequence of uncontrolled *nafs*. Since many of the vices in *Kulliyat* resulted from man succumbing to the temptation of woman's company, her sexuality led to self-indulgence and lack of social responsibility for both.

On the one hand, men and women have both *nafs* and *aql* and are socially evaluated according to how well they conform to Islamic norms and their concern for the *umma*, the community. On the other hand, men and women are intrinsically different in that women are associated with *nafs* which involves a "natural" self-centeredness and inferiority. According to the Ferghanachis, it was for this reason that though both sexes should be modest and should seek to avoid the gaze of strangers of the opposite sex, thereby precluding the spontaneous arousal of *nafs*, it is women who must veil.

In Kunduz, unveiled women were popularly referred to by the Persian phrase *ruy luch* (naked face) with its connotation of immodesty. That these women went about "bare faced" with the permission of their husbands and in-laws was irrelevant. The woman exposing her face would be seen by men and these men might desire the woman. While this was sinful for the men, it was also the sin for the woman whose fault it was for arousing them in the first place. Without the veil, there was no protection for either men or women. The women who were *ruy luch* were bad, but the men who had given them permission were without honor and without social responsibility. They were essentially pimps and procurers (*mordagaw*-Persian) (*dayuz*-Uzbek), one of the worst epithets a man could be called.

This value system, which underlay the appropriate roles given to men and women, led intrinsically to ideas about social responsibility and community life. Because women were likely to indulge in behavior governed by *nafs* rather than *aql*, not only were they to veil but they also were more restricted to the household where their male relatives ensured that their *nafs* did not subvert the social order. Women's tasks therefore revolved around family and the household though they influenced the public arena through reputation and influence over household men. Women's ordinary loyalties and concerns were therefore expressed within their immediate family situation and expanded to the kin network. On the other hand, men's roles were oriented toward the marketplace and the mosque. It was they who expressed their community loyalties in the arena of ethnic political and economic competition. Since they had the opportunity to develop *aql* through religious study and mosque attendance, men also were supposedly more concerned with broader social and political goals, the creation of the good society.

Traditionally women in Central Asia could not go to the bazaar, but brothers and other male relatives made purchases for them (Bacon 1966:70). In Kunduz, the Ferghanachis followed the new urban pattern whereby women occasionally made visits to the bazaar and did their own shopping. Of course, they wore the full length *chadari*, and they asked permission of their husbands, fathers, or in-laws before they went. The veil insured anonymity in the bazaar. Wealth and poverty were hidden along with the personality of the wearer. Within the adjoining lanes of *mahalla* Kasani, people learned to recognize which woman had a certain color *chadari* and the news about who was going where spread quickly. This seeming lack of anonymity was an expansion of the household sphere into the localized community. Women were in *chadari* before most neighborhood men, but they recognized them and relied on them as escorts from night celebrations and as protection against strangers.

The typical symbolic associations of the veil were said to be manipulated and reversed by individual women. Since the veil provided anonymity, it could be used to carry on an affair. The example told to me involved a woman who wished to receive certain bazaar items cheaply. She dressed herself with care, putting on cosmetics as if she were going to a party and went to the shop where she thought to make a deal with the shopkeeper. In the shop, she raised her veil and flirted with the owner. They agreed that she would meet him there, have sexual relations, and in return, would receive goods from the store. Knowledge of the woman's identity in this situation was kept hidden since she wore the veil to and from her assignation. Though not explicitly stated, the reluctance of men to allow their women to go frequently to the bazaar by themselves may have been related to their fears of adulterous affairs.

As might be expected, the women had a somewhat different perspective. For them, it was men and men alone who are governed by insatiable desires, *nafs*. They believed that women were vulnerable and needed protection from men by other men, household kinsmen, or symbolically through the veil. One day while flipping through my Persian-English dictionary, a woman informant came across the word, *shawat*, lust. The informant commented that only men and few evil women are lustful; most women are not. The almost paranoid fear of strangers was perhaps attributable to feelings that men were somehow governed by evil appetites and were therefore beyond control. If a group of men were standing on a corner near the gate to our lane, women would not leave the security of the compound walls even with their veils down. If groups of men were standing on a major street corner where the women usually hired a horsecart to take them to the bazaar, instead of stopping, the women would walk on. When riding in a taxi or horsecart, a male kinsman always sat next to the driver and women sat on the other side of the kinsman and in the back. At the very least as many children as possible were piled between driver and passengers.[7] The fear of men was proportionate to the men's ethnic distance from the woman's own *qawm*. Just as men distrusted women as sexual betrayers, women distrusted men as sexual abusers. Men and women mutually maintained some amount of distrust and separation. The attitudes about sexual betrayal and sexual abuse represented the sex-linked internalizations of the separation of the sexes into two communities.

These attitudes about the other gender reinforced in-group solidarity regarding appropriate marriage partners. A Ferghanachi man said he would be reluctant to marry someone from another ethnic group because he would not know how she was brought up, whether she was modest in the household and veiled outside of it. His lack of knowledge about his in-laws also would lessen his leverage on his wife's behavior. Coupled with this attitude about marrying outsiders was extreme possessiveness about Ferghanachi women. This possessiveness was expressed in fearful statements about other men, especially Pashtuns, seeking to marry *muhajir* girls, "because everyone knows they are the best cooks, and know how to keep the household in proper order." Thus, a man married a woman from his own group to prevent other men from taking her and because he felt that she would not betray him.

Women likewise made judgments that their own men were superior to others, usually including the notion that they were concerned about the household, and bought bazaar goods for the house and family members. Fear of sexual abuse was explicitly related to foreign men's insatiability, frequent desire for sexual intercourse which had to be accommodated, rough treatment, frequent pregnancies, and fear that other wives or prostitutes would be favored.

## The Separation into Gender-based Communities

Children picked up the attitudes about sexuality, womanhood, and manhood from parents as they expressed or acted out feelings about their own lives and their expectations regarding their sons and daughters. Then, when children thought of the adult social world, they perceived it from their own gender position. Boys knew they would become members of the male adult community and girls would become members of the female adult community.

Paralleling the gender ideology, the gender-based community structure meant that behavioral norms were under the direction of either the men's or women's community. Emotional support was provided to individuals by the groups, men to men, and women to women.

In the anthropological discussion of traditional Mediterranean values which are also applied to the Middle East, the dual conception of honor and shame is held to be the mainstay of proper conduct. For the Ferghanachis, male honor was imbued with ideals based on Islamic religious knowledge. Quranic ideals were used to judge individuals. Secondarily, involvement in the community, help and attendance in community celebrations, participation in community decision-making, and concern for the maintenance of the *muhajirs* as an ethnic entity were standards by which men were judged.

A man in his thirties with a wife and children often began to take on an increasing role in community affairs. He sought to become a leader of the men's community. Before the emigration from Central Asia, mosque officials and other men who became influential passed down a certain dimension of power to their sons. However, the emigration disrupted the transmission because many came into Afghanistan without their parents and without inherited resources. By the 1970s, the reorganized community contained Afghan-born sons just of the age to begin the quest for community position. Many were to take important roles in the resistance movement against the Marxist government.

According to community belief, leadership positions were earned. The community leader of *mahalla* Kasani as of the late 1970s, Abdur Rahman, the *mawlewi* of the local mosque, did not pass on his position to his eldest son because the son took no interest in community affairs even before the change of government in 1978 disrupted community life. On the other hand, Harun, the son of the second most important leader in the *mahalla*, A. A., was considered bright and involved in community affairs. He eventually became the Ferghanachi's first martyr when he was killed by the Taraki regime shortly after the coup.

Wealth was a criterion for leadership that informants tended to downplay, since the two community leaders were not the richest people in the *mahalla*. Still, men would usually admit that a certain amount of wealth was necessary, because leaders were supposed to entertain more guests, including outsiders, in a lavish manner.

The two recognized community leaders were both mosque officials, but they took on slightly different roles vis-a-vis the *qawm* community and the Kunduz population. Mawlewi Abdur Rahman's activities were more political: he served as advisor to local non-Ferghanachi Uzbek groups in land settlement disputes and was widely known as an elected representative to the national assembly during the constitutional period. Despite Abdur Rahman's higher official position in the Kasani mosque, it was the other man A. A. who was more often cited as the religious authority for the *muhajirs*. He was viewed as the stricter of the two men with regard to interpreting proper Muslim conduct. Thus, young men who wanted to wear longer hair and mustaches following Pashtun and Kabuli style were reprimanded by A. A., not by Abdur Rahman. Many Kasanis refused to go out and see the carnival and festive sights on New Year's Day since that day was a secular

*Photo 5.3  Kasani mosque in Kunduz*

and not religiously sanctioned celebration, and A. A. had allegedly said going was contrary to Islam. This division of labor among the leadership of the Kasani community was due to personality factors of the two men and possibly to the ethnic and political situation which endured in Kunduz until 1978.

A brief account of Abdur Rahman's experience in the national assembly election demonstrates the conflicts of community duty, wealth, and personal conduct in the life of a leader. Leaders of the Uzbek, Tajik, and *muhajir* communities in Kunduz requested that he run for national assembly. His major opponent was the son of an influential Pashtun. The preparations and elections were said to cost him 120,000 afghanis in personal expenses. Trucks had to be hired and sent to bring in village Uzbeks and Tajiks to vote. At that time, the gas agreement with the Soviet Union had terminated, and the price of gas had quickly doubled. Many of these voters were housed in the Kasani mosque, others in the private guesthouses of the *mahalla*, and all had to be fed.

During his term, the *mawlewi* was naturally expected to do favors for his constituents in their dealings with the government ministries. Using bribery in these deals as an influence broker was common practice. However, Abdur Rahman felt that this practice violated correct religious behavior and he refused to participate using such methods. He also felt that the Kabuli lifestyle was detrimental to the religious life. Therefore, at re-election time he declined to run again.

Only after a man was perhaps fifty years old was the concern which he demonstrated for the past fifteen years or twenty years rewarded in influence and prestige. Even community leaders had no direct sanctions at their disposal to insure that their wishes were not overlooked. Community gossip and subtle verbal attack were the chief methods used in community control. Thus, in a small quick wedding, Abdur Rahman was not consulted on the arrangements. In this case, other old men also were not involved. To show their disapproval of the family who disregarded the conventions of proper conduct regarding community elders, the elders simply did not attend the wedding. A man told me that of the twenty-five old men one would normally expect to see at a celebration, only ten showed up. Naturally, this created a good deal of talk about the wedding family in the community at large. This man further explained that later Abdur Rahman or another of these old men might say publicly to a member of the wedding family that he did not attend because he was tired or another excuse that everyone present would know was untrue. Public humiliation served as a warning to others not to behave similarly.

All adult men participated in community decisions along with the *mahalla* leadership during meetings held in the community mosque after the first or last daily prayer. According to male informants, at these meetings, the *mawlewi* always talked first, but afterwards any man, Ferghanachi or non-Ferghanachi, young or old, was free to participate at will. The ideas of any participant could be adopted. Thus, in the discussion of a new building within the mosque grounds for a religious school, the process of construction, builder, materials, and design were unsettled questions. Finally, the men adopted a suggestion of a Tajik originally from Chahar Darra village that the Kunduz municipality architect be called in to draw a blueprint.

For men, the bazaar and the mosque replaced yearly and life crisis celebrations as focal points of interest. Thus, men were involved in social relations which included a wider ethnic variety. As important as these social relations were, they seldom involved ritual or symbolic activities nor did these relationships breach compound walls. Community affairs publicly conducted in the mosque allowed men the opportunity to express opinions, to judge and be judged.

Women, perhaps because they were more confined to the household, marked more occasions with special celebrations than did men. Births and weddings included a series of ritual celebrations to which there were no male equivalents. Even the celebration of the Islamic holidays such as after Ramadan were considered to be woman's pleasure. There was a saying that women celebrate the holiday for seven days and some male joker usually added not seven days but fourteen. Since women were busy preparing food for male guests, and made new clothes for their family, their own holiday visits were put off until afterward. There was indeed a greater frequency of female visiting for a few days after a major holiday or celebration. It was necessary at such times to visit kin, see how the new brides in the area were getting along, and find out other news.

Decisions about future marriages, control of young women by elders, judgments of morality and sin, gossip and exchange of information all took place when women gathered. At the celebrations themselves, women made use of symbolic acts to express their community. At each celebration, every woman was given a small embroidered handkerchief as a remembrance. Women employed a prolonged set of greeting and farewell rituals and in every way symbolically embellished the social bonds that connected them.

Margaret Fallers described the separation of men and women in Turkey:

> For young girls it [the separate life] means being included in the tasks of the household, learning the wide range of skills necessary to be a working member of a group of women keeping house. And it means being judged by women on one's ability to preserve food, roll dough, pickle olives, sew, dance, manage small children and appear respectfully pious. For growing girls, it means learning modest, discreet behavior appropriate in public so as not to attract the attention of non-family men, and thus the scolding of older women (1976:252).

While not exact in particulars, the Ferghanachi women's community functioned similarly. Judgments were made on the performance of household tasks at home and through women's rituals. The shame portion of the honor/shame duo was operative. And women themselves were its enforcing agents. An immodest girl or woman would lose her position in the women's community; she was an object of reproach, and her outlet of sociability with peers was accordingly lessened.

Unlike the men's community where secular leadership and religious authority were for the most part combined, in the women's community these were functionally separated. The leaders were those who gave advice, participated in the organization of women's gatherings, were active in wedding arrangements, and were looked to as judges of moral conduct. Religious specialists, the *bibi mullahs*, were not necessarily authority figures though they were respected for their knowledge.

Parallel to the structure of community leadership was a respect system based primarily on age. Young married men aged twenty-five to forty began participation in community affairs, earned respect through religious conduct and correct social behavior; middle-aged men, forty to sixty years old, reached a stage in which their special skills were known and respected. Old age, especially after sixty-three, the age Mohammed died, was a special category. Respect was given to these people on the basis of age alone. All those in this category were viewed as community elders to be consulted and honored, but the words of a few men, the leaders, were separated out and venerated even above the rest. Within *mahalla* Kasani, all the Kasani elders were called or referred to by respect titles, at the least *haji* since most made the *haj*, or almost as often *qari* for their study and memorization of the Quran.

The respect system was symbolically expressed at each celebration through the seating arrangement. In a rectangular room, the wall farthest from the door was reserved for elders. The oldest men were ushered to this area by the others in the room. The leaders themselves were seated in the corner farthest from the door. The greatest delicacies were always put in front of the elders, and special gifts were presented to them whatever the occasion. In winter when a *sandali* was in the room, the elders were seated around the sandali. The next lower age group, forty to sixty year olds, made up the majority of invited guests at most celebration meals. They were seated down the lengths of the room. It was not considered proper to push oneself forward closest to the wall of elders. Instead, one should constantly insist that newer arrivals sit "above" one's own position. Still, the arrangement generally worked out so that increasing age governed placement. Young marrieds sat nearest the door. Usually unmarried boys held their own celebration in another room, if, in fact, there were unmarried guests.

# NOTES

1. The boy was circumcised at a men's celebration. Chagatay and Sjoberg (1955:92) report age 1-2 as age of circumcision for Kabul *muhajirs*. Snesarev (1972, 10 (3):276) reports 5, 7, or 9 for rural Uzbeks historically.

2. Snesarev (1972, 10 (3):265) reports white, including a white wedding dress, as the dominant color symbolism of Uzbek weddings.

3. Female beauty was defined as round face, fair complexion, dark eyes, brows, and hair, and soft rounded figure.

4. Most Ferghanachi babies were vaccinated against smallpox at the family services clinic. Unofficially, the last big smallpox epidemic in Kunduz was in the 1950s. Many informants said they had lost children then.

5. M. J. Good (1977) points out that in Iran, women disliked the pill because they felt it caused them to age. Spotting between periods from the pill also spoiled ritual purity.

6. Much sexual humor was made of similar analogies between food and sex. For example, one little girl did not like carrots and picked them out of her *pilaw*. A woman jokingly explained that virgins should not eat carrots; the joke being a reference to the penis as a carrot and sexual intercourse. Another joke was referring to baby girls as *pista bazaar*, pistachio nuts, because their genitals were said to resemble the nuts.

7. I took the male role and was frequently a buffer between women and drivers. I placed children between myself and the driver when possible.

# Chapter 6

## Islam and Ethnicity

That Islam was crucial to the Ferghanachis has been indicated in previous chapters, for example, in the structuring of daily life by the five divisions of required prayer, in the attitudes related to gender taught via Persian Islamic texts in the mosque schools, in the idea that honor and leadership given to a man were based upon his religious knowledge and authority, and that the secular New Year's celebration was to be avoided. The clearest expression of Islamic norms in personal and interpersonal value judgments appeared in household or neighborhood social situations (Shalinsky 1990). Young and old, men and women should behave according to an appropriate standard, informants said. Significantly, the standards were perceived as deriving from one source, Islam.

As emigrants from Soviet Central Asia, many of the community thought of themselves as having made *hijrat*. Adherence to Islam therefore was part of the consciously chosen identity which had historical roots for this group. Many individuals had also incorporated this into their personal identity and retained names from towns in Soviet Central Asia which they considered their true homeland.[1]

That religious responsibilities were taken seriously is indicated in the following two examples from observations and interview data:

> A young married woman was so busy doing household chores that she neglected to perform the afternoon prayer. Since she was alone in her household (except for me), the omission could have been passed over with none the wiser, but the woman was very upset, in tears, wondering whether this omission would harm any of the housework she had completed. When her father-in-law arrived home, she confessed the omission. He advised that she perform extra prayers during the next period. She became much calmer at his words.

Clearly, this woman was not only concerned about social conformity since no one was present to enforce the rules. She did however integrate her personal beliefs with all of her behavior. The religious duty of prayer affected her other household activities. She judged herself harshly.

> A young man, mid-teens, of the household where I was living told me not long after my arrival that it was acceptable that I eat rice from the same

platter as the rest of the family. Since I had previously been doing this, I was puzzled by his bringing up this issue as a problem. He explained that there had been a discussion of this by the religious leaders at the local mosque. They concluded that since Americans were believers with a holy book [they thought all Americans were Christians], they could participate in a meal with Muslims. Of course Russians who are atheists could not ever eat with Muslims, said the boy.

This boy had obviously been concerned about the issue of my eating with the family. He was relieved that it was acceptable. Clearly part of the boy's reaction was socially motivated. He did not want his family to feel the wrath of the religious leaders and community ostracism. Yet he was also concerned that he do the right thing personally. The conversation also illustrated attitudes about the Soviets who likewise were judged for their attitudes concerning religion.

Like the majority of Muslims in Afghanistan, the *muhajirs* were followers of the Sunni tradition, Hanafi rite. Many were eager to instruct a potential convert in the tenets of Islam. *Shahadat,* the profession of faith that there is no god but God and that Mohammed is His messenger, was taken seriously as the way in which an individual identified himself as Muslim. For this reason, several people sporadically attempted to "trick" me into saying this until it almost became like a game. By having me repeat one syllable at a time or asking if I would read some calligraphy, they sought a lasting conversion for my own good. In fact, one of the last things the "grandfather" of the household where I lived said with tears in his eyes was, "If only you would stay and become a Muslim, it would truly have been a perfect time." When another American visited the household and readily said the profession of faith, he was embraced by some Muslim visitors from a different ethnic group. But the "grandfather" left the room and refused to eat with him because he did not trust one who professed faith so easily. The sincerity of the grandfather's motivation was striking. As illustrated in this example of a "foreigner's conversion," judgments made about people using Islamic tests are complex since not only the outward behavior but also the inner self should be taken into account.

In the neighborhood community, the five prayer times were rigorously observed. They performed two *rak'at,* prayer units, commanded by God (*farz*) and two commanded by Mohammed (*sunnat*) at daybreak; at noon, four *farz* and six *sunnat*; before sunset, four *farz*; after sunset, three *farz* and two *sunnat*; and before retiring, four *farz* and two *sunnat*. They also performed three *wajib* or other obligatory prayer units as part of the last prayer. This represented substantial commitment to prayer.

Children as young as four or five began to imitate the bowing movements of their parents. Girls began the prayer obligation at ten or eleven and boys generally later. Only men attended the mosque. Women prayed at home. Prayer etiquette was observed. At the individual rose from the embroidered prayer cloth, he or she formally greeted the others in the room. During the prayer itself, no one was to walk in front of the cloth, blocking the individual from Mecca.

Sometimes when friends or newlyweds prayed side by side in the household, laughter and jokes would invalidate the prayer set. Thus the norms were occasionally violated and adherence to the strict prayer rules was partially socially motivated. It was very rare for any individual to be completely alone at prayer. Other members of the household or visitors were likely to be present. Gossip about lack of religious observance could damage family prestige in the community.

Some individuals emphasized the individual's inner feeling in his/her approach to God during prayer. These feelings possibly were residual effects of Naqshbandi sufism, which was a major social and political force in Central Asia when the emigrant generation was growing into adulthood.

Certain notions of morality held by some people such as prohibitions against too much music and dance perhaps had an origin in Central Asia sufism, as Eugene Schuyler reported in 1877 for the Khanate of Kokand (II:28). Though some considered it decadent, by the mid 1970s it had become fashionable for hired women to sing and play musical instruments at women's marriage celebrations rather than women merely entertaining themselves by dancing to the accompaniment of the *daira*, a tambourine-like drum. This innovation was deprecated by those who considered paid female entertainers to be the equivalent of prostitutes. These people considered music and dancing to promote lascivious behavior. During the fieldwork period only two women from Khanabad, who performed with their children, were allowed to play music at the neighborhood weddings but the innovators spoke of their hopes to bring entertainment from Kabul, the Afghan capital. The controversy indicated that it was precisely over such issues as community morality in which the conflict between what were perceived as Islamic standards and "modern" values was played out.

A more obvious conflict between Islamic rules for behavior and western values concerned the use of alcoholic beverages. Some informants categorically stated that Uzbeks never drank alcohol. What they meant was that as good Muslims, Uzbeks could never drink alcohol. Yet there were men's celebrations in which alcohol brought up from Kabul was consumed. In Kabul at the time it is likely that some *muhajir* Uzbeks had abandoned Islamic practice in regard to alcohol consumption.

Morality stories were told by many to illustrate ideas of right and wrong. In this story which allegedly was true and occurred in the mid 1960s, a wicked man in a position of authority as a judge, a state-appointed position under the Ministry of Justice, repeatedly violated Islamic standards of character.

> The *qazi* (judge) had one wife who died, leaving a daughter. He then married the older of two sisters. As is common, the younger sister often visited the household. Unknown to the older sister, during these visits the younger had sexual relations with the *qazi*. Eventually, she was given to a good boy in marriage. When the boy went to have sex with her for the first time, he noticed she had a big stomach. She told him that she had a pain there. Actually, she was six months pregnant. The *qazi* remained at the house with the bride and groom and finally kicked the boy out, telling him that the girl was his. Three months later when the child was born, the *qazi* put it to sleep naked under the woodstove, cooked it to death, and buried it in the yard. From that time on, he and the younger sister slept in one house in the compound and the older sister . . . slept in another house in the compound.
>
> The two sisters had a brother . . . This man threatened his brother-in-law, indicating that he should give up the younger sister but the *qazi* refused to take the threats seriously. One night, the brother was let into the compound by the older sister. As the *qazi* returned from work and the younger sister went out to embrace him, dressed in the fine clothes he had given her, the brother shot them both five time as they stood together, and they both died . . .

The *qazi* demonstrated many horrible sins in this account, seducing his wife's sister, interfering in a legitimate marriage, killing his own child, treating his "wives" unequally and not repenting of his bad behavior. Much of his sinful behavior was directly in violation of Quranic law and he did pay the appropriate price.

According to informants all behavior was classified into sinful or rewarded categories. There were several intermediate categories: behavior strictly neutral; behavior considered good but not rewarded by God; and behavior not sinful but not to be indulged in often. The *qazi's* behavior was obviously sinful; watching dog, bird, and camel fighting, wrestling and games of chance are not sinful, but they are not to be indulged in. Watching *buzkashi*, or *ulaq* (Uzbek), the traditional Uzbek and Turkmen horseback sport played at wedding and circumcision celebrations, falls into the same category.

A young man once emphasized in a conversation that he had lived in northern Afghanistan his entire life and yet he had never and would never attend *buzkashi*. According to one religious authority of the community, the Quran prohibits a man from putting himself in the way of death, suicide. Attending *buzkashi* involved spectators with men who were "in the way of death" since fighting over a cow carcass and transporting it to a goal invited serious injury in the mad scuffling of men and horses. Viewing the spectacle was not sinful, but was not good conduct. The *buzkashi* rider committed a sin each time he participated. For *muhajir* Uzbek men to avoid *buzkashi* completely was unusual, but the knowledge of the Islamic norms for behavior illustrated a social control mechanism which prevented a man from ignoring his proper social responsibilities and overindulging in games and sports.

One old *chapandaz* (*buzkashi* rider) who made the pilgrimage to Mecca, aware of his sin, availed himself of the means through which a sin can be cleansed, the vow of repentance. This man, a village Uzbek, before entering the holy city, vowed never again to participate in *buzkashi*. Then cleansed of his past, he completed the pilgrimage.[2] The vow, particularly sickbed and deathbed repentance, was a highly honorable behavioral form. Often it served to heal family conflict in addition to renewing personal religious and moral convictions.

Those who made the pilgrimage to Mecca were welcomed back into the community with a celebration known as *Haji Chaqirdi* (Haji welcoming). Candies and coins were thrown over the pilgrim as he or she entered the celebration. This same custom was done in all rites of passage and indicated the community's recognition of the person in the new status. The *haji* distributed gifts bought in Mecca including the precious water from the well of Zum Zum which saved the life of Ishmael, Abraham's son.

Religious practice was primarily a matter of daily routine broken up by some celebrations. The daily routine shifted somewhat for the month-long fast of Ramadan in which people abstained from eating and drinking. During Ramadan, women did housework at night and the big meal was eaten before dawn. For the three-day celebration after Ramadan, people wore new clothes and children were given small gifts or coins. Alms were given to the poor. Though the alms were felt to be of the greatest religious significance, the celebrations also included much social visiting which reinforced kinship relations, neighborhood association and friendship groups based on gender, age, and respect patterns.

On a less important religious occasion, *Mawlud*, the anniversary of the Prophet Mohammed's birth, the neighborhood community sometimes decided to give a *khayrat*, a special distribution of food to thank God and gain His reward. Families contributed money which was used to purchase food, rice, cooking oil, meat, carrots, raisins, candies and tea. The mosque courtyard was the location for the food preparation, and the poor from the town who heard of the distribution went there to eat and to get portions to take home to their families. Some of the needy visited households on a regular basis for clothing and other items. On *Mawlud*, giving to the poor was considered particularly appropriate. Each family who gave money for the *khayrat* received a platter of *pilaw* for use in the household. Thus the community almsgiving also served as a community feast.

The Ferghanachis' conception of Islam incorporated a complex integration between personal religious belief, behavior and group norms. Clearly in the urban context of northern Afghanistan in the 1970s, the five pillars of Islam, the profession of faith, prayer, almsgiving, the fast of Ramadan and the pilgrimage to Mecca were extremely important to the overwhelming majority of people. Rites of passage including circumcision for boys, marriage, and funerals also universally had an Islamic component.

## Islam and Interethnic Conflict

In the complex interethnic arena of a provincial capital like Kunduz, changing values and Islamic standards became a way of organizing ethnic competition. Ethnic prestige was partially based upon a group's reputation for knowing and observing Islam. In a discussion of bride price with some non-*muhajir* Uzbeks, they indicated some of the complexity of judging ethnic prestige. On the one hand, the average bride price of their Uzbek group was higher than that of the Ferghanachis of Kunduz. Therefore in discussion of this topic, they stated their superiority. On the other hand, they also said that the Ferghanachi way was better and their explanation was that it demonstrated more concern with proper religious values and less concern with money and possessions. Thus an Islamic reputation balanced out economic and social inferiority to a certain extent.

On another occasion, I visited a Pashtun family in the neighborhood who represented the economically and politically dominant ethnic group in Afghanistan. After several hours, the owner of the house where I lived, came to their compound door, refrained from entering since they were women alone, and sent a message in with a boy to fetch me home. They immediately rose to do his bidding and commented on how praiseworthy these people were to be so religiously observant and to know so well the proper way to behave. These same Pashtuns thought it was a great scandal when these Uzbeks arranged a marriage with a Persian-speaking group known as Arabs who had an impious reputation.

Still, even these Arabs used the same kind of Islamic tests. One day the Arab groom's grandfather went into the neighborhood mosque courtyard and accused his grandson's bride's uncle, an important religious authority, of promoting religious laxity by permitting a woman entertainer at the marriage celebrations. In that instance the man's own ungenerous character left him open to the accusation that he was unwilling to pay for a good celebration and thus the Islamic test backfired (Shalinsky 1980).

Another example in which knowledge of Islam was played out in interethnic competition occurred one evening in a Pashtun village near Kabul. A teenage Ferghanachi boy and I were invited by another American to the house of a well-educated Pashtun. The Pashtun initiated the conversation by asking the boy about religion in northern Afghanistan. He stated that he had heard that Uzbeks always received new clothes in honor of the New Year. The boy replied that only on the festival after Ramadan and the celebration commemorating Abraham's sacrifice did those in his group receive new clothes but perhaps his host's custom was different. The host denied that his group wore new clothes on the New Year. The host then asked the boy if he had ever visited the Tomb of Ali, a common custom of the New Year's celebration, and the boy replied that he had not. The tones of both were scrupulously polite as befitted the rules of hospitality. The conversation between the boy and the Pashtun indicated that each was aware that March 21, the secular New Year in Afghanistan, was not celebrated by those religiously observant. This idea, which was not shared by all Afghans, provided a mechanism by which an individual indicated religious superiority;  one's group was set apart from the masses who were ignorant of Islam. Ferghanachi men were skilled at handling these interethnic situations. Women generally were held to a less rigorous religious standard and were even permitted to have a special party around New Year's time during which they distributed a special food of sprouted wheat juice, *sumulak.*

*Photo 6.1 Buzkashi riders*

Islam's importance was essential in the personal internalized value system manifested in daily behavior, the social network localized in the neighborhood with the mosque providing leadership, and the arena of interethnic controlled conflict played out locally and nationally. Within these three contexts, Islam served as a filter through which ideas and behavior were selected and judged. Since Islamic-based observance and judgment were internalized by individuals but were not exclusively personal, Islam contained a social and political element which potentially provided a powerful force for stability or change as witnessed in the resistance movement to the Marxist government.

## Ethnic Attitudes and Relationships

While Sunni Islam provided a source of unity for Afghanistan, ethnic diversity reinforced social divisions. In the Afghanistan of the 1970s, particularly for urbanites who constantly faced multi-ethnic social situations, it was acceptable for people to ask and be asked their ethnic affiliation. Sometimes *qawm* was asked but occasionally the broader Persian term *mardom*, people, was used to ask ethnic group. While each individual made his own choice in a given situation, his choice was limited to the hierarchy of ethnic labels that coincided with other symbols of ethnicity, particularities of dress, food preference, occupation, residence pattern. Each of these worked together to bound the available possibilities unless the individual's choice was a denial expressed by the adoption of symbolic forms of other groups.

For the Ferghanachis the range of responses available was great. They could respond with the name of the town origin group, Kasanis, Tashkendis, etc., which referred to only a hundred or so households, they could respond with the term, *muhajir*, with its religious and historical connotation and thereby identity with those from Ferghana or Bukhara, possibly over a hundred thousand people, or they could respond with the label of an even larger group of over a million speakers, the Uzbeks.

The choice of the town origin group was most likely to occur in a situation in which both parties in the conversation were *muhajirs*, yet the individuals were not known to each other. In this context, a man was asked his father and his father's occupation also. A name deriving from the town of origin was attached to the personal name as an identifying feature. Thus, I saw a businessman's official stationery used for his import-export transactions with the surname Kasani. Those born in Afghanistan used the same appellation. Thus, a Ferghanachi born in Afghanistan told me to refer to him in my book with the surname Kasani. Never did anyone indicate that he was to be called after the town of Kunduz. Occasionally, young persons under twenty years of age vehemently insisted that

Afghanistan, more specifically Kunduz, was the *watan*, homeland. But their parents corrected them, saying that the watan was *Shurawi*, the Soviet Union.[3]

Most commonly, the response given when identity questions were asked was the simple explanation "from the other side," which referred to the other side of the river, Amu Darya. Members of other ethnic groups were unaware of the subtler distinctions which differentiated the Tashkendi from the Kasani, or the Andijani from the Samarkandi. Thus, people from other ethnic groups used the term, Ferghanachi or Bukharai, lumping together all those who were immigrants.

When I accompanied women informants to the park, the whispers of others could be heard that the foreigner looked like a Ferghanachi, since I was wearing homemade clothes. When I went to the family planning clinic with some women, again I was pointed out, "There is a foreigner who looks like the Ferghanachis." Then one of the more daring of the women asked one of my informants, "Can she understand your language?" referring to Uzbek which my friends were using to converse so they could not be understood. (The response was, "Ask her yourself, she speaks Persian," which effectively ended the conversation about me.) Interestingly, Uzbek speech was associated with the Ferghanachis in this situation. The criterion of language usage was ambiguous since Ferghanachi traditional bilingualism operated as a two-way differentiating factor when observed by outsiders. Thus, the Persian speakers at the family planning clinic differentiated themselves by emphasizing the Uzbek speech of the Ferghanachis. On the other hand, Afghan Uzbeks in Ferghanachi neighborhoods in Kunduz differentiated themselves by emphasizing the Persian speech of their Ferghanachi neighbors. Once, an Andkhoi Uzbek woman asked me rhetorically, "The Ferghanachis speak *farsi* (Persian) at home, don't they?" She tended to view their significant language as Persian, thinking the switch to Uzbek in her presence was due to politeness or a recognition of Uzbek superiority.

When a person answered the identity question with "from the other side," he essentially made a distinction between Afghan native and non-native. This response had overt political implications which were readily commented on by informants. Discrimination in property disputes and other difficulties in dealing with government bureaucrats were laid at the door of Pashtun indifference and/or hostility to non-natives. Though they deprecated their "second class status" in Afghanistan, immigrant background had become a focal point of resistance to Pashtun dominance. While theoretically there were native Tajiks and Uzbeks as well as immigrant Tajiks and Uzbeks, the native/non-native distinction was fused with the Pashtun/non-Pashtun distinction by most politically aware Ferghanachi men. The fusion of the two distinctions was augmented by the fact that to the overwhelming majority of all ethnic groups in Afghanistan, including Pashtuns,

Afghan meant Pashtun. As one informant succinctly put it, the very name of this country, Afghanistan, land of the Afghans, is an insult to us.

Ferghanachi, the most common label used by outsiders, was resented by some informants because they believed it pointed to the native/non-native distinction. Their attitude was thus inconsistent but clear. They were allowed to refer to themselves as emigrants, yet no one else was. Actually, informants said that the public use of Ferghanachi in their presence was formerly unusual. It seemed to have lost some of its power as an insult and was heard on public occasions in inter-ethnic exchange. I heard a hired woman musician from Khanabad address the women at a wedding: "Oh Ferghanachis, what is the matter with you? Why aren't you giving me money?" The custom was to pay the hired musician in small amounts in praise of various guests who took turns dancing. In this case, the use of the term Ferghanachi was considered amusing. Those who heard the woman smiled and one said to me, "Did you hear her call the Ferghanachis so she can be paid?"

Most women and some Ferghanachi men did not have the next level of response in their repertoire. To identify with the larger groups of Uzbeks or Tajiks meant that an individual disregarded two of the most important criteria of the previous labels. First, the consideration of endogamy as a group boundary mechanism disappeared. The Uzbeks or Tajiks included many groups which were themselves endogamous. Marriage with an Uzbek or Tajik who was not of one's group would formally be said to be not as bad as marrying, for example, a Pashtun, but informants generally considered it equivalent to marrying a stranger with the resulting loss of a group member.[4] Second, the common historical dilemma shared by *muhajirs*, the abandonment of the homeland, was lost when the term Uzbek or Tajik was used as self-definition. An individual who chose to identify with the larger groups lost even the significant native/non-native distinction.

Informants who did use the Uzbek label were young men, usually with a high school education. Often they were educated either at Kabul University or at one of the local teacher training institutes. The broader experience in interaction with outsiders led to a heightened political consciousness in many cases. It was these men who formed study groups and literary groups for Uzbek language work. They purchased records and tapes of classical Central Asian music. They were aware of domestic political currents which in certain times were more liberal to the expressions of ethnic consciousness by minorities.

The Uzbek identity itself contained elements which led it to be chosen over Tajik. Uzbeks were the rulers of northern Afghanistan and the ruling dynasties in the three emirates of Central Asia. They were known as warriors while Tajiks were considered pacific. For whatever reason, the choice of Uzbek identity over the Tajik was the regular pattern for Ferghanachi men who chose to make this level of response to identity questions. Even when individuals had no personal justification for their use of the Uzbek identity, as in the case of the Kasanis who came from a Tajik town, they claimed they were Uzbeks anyway. Perhaps, there was recognition that Uzbek speech operated as ethnic boundary and shared ethnic tradition. Those who spoke Uzbek, whether native or immigrant, shared a distinct cultural pattern. Though recognizing the different groups within the larger Uzbek unit, the men who chose to identify with the larger unit felt a connection with other Uzbeks. Whether it was the common political reaction to Pashtun dominance or some shared semantic structuring of the universe, two men who found they spoke Uzbek trusted each other more readily. The only workmen that would be hired to work within Ferghanachi household compounds were other Uzbeks. When I asked the identity of the plasterers or carpenters brought into the compound, they turned out to be from some Uzbek group. When the household in which I lived sold a male calf, it was to a special friend of the family, a village Uzbek.

Perhaps the most amusing example of the adoption of individuals within the Uzbek label was that I became one myself. One night I was to meet some other Americans up from Kabul in a Kunduz teahouse. I went accompanied by a male informant. There were quite a few foreigners in the teahouse as it was New Year's time and they had come for the *buzkashi* tournament. While I went to have some papers signed by an American official, saving me a trip to Kabul, my informant as he told me later was approached by a village Uzbek. The Uzbek said that he was an Uzbek and could tell that the man he was addressing was also an Uzbek. My informant granted that this was a correct assumption. Then the Uzbek continued, "I saw the woman you are with and I know she is an Uzbek." The informant started to explain that I was actually a foreigner, but the other still insisted that I was Uzbek. The informant was so amused that he decided to agree. Encouraged, the village man decided to pick out others in the teahouse among the foreigners and confirm with his new acquaintance that they were Uzbeks. He picked out an American woman of Japanese descent as his next choice. However, I then returned to the table and ended his game. Apparently, the village man assumed that all countries are ethnically organized in the same way as Afghanistan and thus all had Uzbeks who were recognizable by appearance and behavior. My Uzbek identity was found to be very amusing yet appropriate by others who were told the story by the informant.[5]

That the label was considered appropriate was an indication of group acceptance based on my physical appearance and behavior. Informants made judgments about ethnic behaviors with Uzbeks receiving the highest marks. Informants made statements like: Uzbeks do not beat their wives; Uzbeks do not drink (alcohol). They expressed the moral superiority of the Uzbeks through definitions of correct behavior.

The Tajik identity was never assumed by my informants when they were asked identity questions. They occasionally identified others as Ferghana Tajiks. Those so identified were usually completely Persian-speaking. Though they understood the Uzbek language, they replied in Persian, never using Uzbek speech themselves. Despite this difference they were completely circumscribed within the endogamous Ferghanachi community. The Ferghanachis were identified as Tajiks on official government documents including citizenship cards and marriage certificates. The government bureaucracy possibly preferred to list most people as Tajiks without even ascertaining origin. Perhaps when the immigrants first sought identity cards, it was a safer identity to assume and later younger men avowed the Uzbek identity.

## Ethnic Relations

In northern Afghanistan, in addition to Uzbeks and Tajiks, there were Turkmens, Kazakhs, and Kirghiz, who had come from Central Asia. Not much was said by Ferghanachis about the Kirghiz, who seldom left their home in the Pamir mountains, although the Kasanis remembered the old days when they had close relations with some Kirghiz since Kasan bordered Kirghizia. For the Turkmens the vast majority were twentieth century immigrants into northern Afghanistan (Slobin 1976:12). The Turkmens had named tribal groups and mixed little with other peoples. So-called ethnic aloofness, Turkmen separation from other northern groups, was also indicated in the stereotypic judgments made about them by others. The judgments, uniformly negative, were that Turkmen were alcohol and opium users and that they mistreated their women, forcing them to work all day on carpets. My women informants were particularly negative about the Turkmens' alleged propensity to marry polygynously. They feared Turkmens as lustful evil men. Some women thought an Uzbek man from Andkhoi in one lane of *mahalla* Kasani was a Turkmen. They insisted that they could not understand his speech when they overheard it, that he was ugly like a Turkmen, and above all, that I should never visit the Andkhoi household when he was there. The man by his own word was an Uzbek and was viewed as an Uzbek by the men of the neighborhood. The significant fact was the extreme form of the expressed fear of Turkmen men. On only one occasion was a Turkmen a guest in the household where I lived. The guest was a schoolboy, a friend of the third son. The two ate together in the guesthouse. Even the Andkhoi Uzbek women, who were from an area of much greater Turkmen population, had never attended a Turkmen wedding celebration. The Kasani women did know a Buhkaran woman married to a Kabuli Turkmen. This woman, her kin, and they were involved in the reciprocal exchange of invitations to large-scale celebrations. But there was no connection between the woman's husband, his natal kin, and the Kasanis, except that of reputation. He was known to be a rich businessman with a house in Paghman, a summer resort town near Kabul. The most frequent contact between Ferghanachi men and Turkmens were bazaar relations, the Turkmens having the carpet selling shops in the Kunduz bazaar. The Turkmen language and Uzbek spoken by my informants were mutually intelligible and used in business transactions.

The case of the Kazakhs was more complex. There were many fewer Kazakhs than either Uzbek or Tajik *muhajirs*. Perhaps the distance from the Kazakh homeland to the Afghan border was prohibitive. Slobin reports that in Mazar-i Sharif, the Kazakhs were in charge of *chapan* sales, a typical *muhajir* occupation (1976:17). My informants could not decide if the Kazakhs were always included under the *muhajir* label. Certainly, as one man pointed out, they were all from the other side, yet as another commented, they used another label and were always called Kazakh by others. Because of the small numbers of Kazakh emigrants, they were not immediately thought of when the term *muhajir* was used. Yet because of their special relations with the Uzbek immigrants, they made up a unique subset of the immigrant community. In Kunduz, many Kazakhs lived in a particular neighborhood which was also home to many Uzbek *muhajirs*. The two groups within the neighborhood had close reciprocal relations; the Kazakhs were invited to the celebrations, weddings, circumcisions, of the Uzbeks, and the Uzbeks were invited to the Kazakh celebrations. Social relations were developed within both the male and female communities. In *mahalla* Kasani, one Ferghanachi was married to a Kazakh woman. The woman was sickly and did not come out of her household much, but she was involved in the core community of the *mahalla* which was dominated by the Kasanis. At the marriage of her son, the Kasani women took the lead in the celebrations, welcoming the bride and her relations to the household. The Kazakh woman was invited to all but the smallest gatherings held by her Kasani neighbors.

The Kasani women looked down upon the Kazakhs rather as poor relations. In their view, the more Mongoloid appearance of the Kazakhs with their high prominent cheekbones, seemingly flattened noses, and epicanthic eyefolds made them ugly. In face-to-face encounters, they were always treated politely. Kazakh and Ferghana Uzbek were mutually intelligible; there was no communication difficulty between the two groups. However, many Kazakhs could not speak Persian and had difficulty in speaking with the more Persian-speaking Ferghanachis.

Slobin reports (1976:104) that the Kazakhs are generally at lower socio-economic levels than the *muhajir* Uzbeks. To give a concrete example, one Ferghanachi family had entered into a patron-client type of relationship with a particular Kazakh family. Several years ago, a Kazakh boy was injured in an automobile accident. The eldest son of the Ferghanachi family got the boy a job as a janitor in the boy's high school. The boy was the sole economic support of his aged mother. Though their household was across town, a thirty-minute walk away, the boy's mother came once a month to pay her respects to the female members of this Ferghanachi family to whom she owed her sustenance. Even in the dead of winter, she came on her periodic visits, never wearing a *chadari*, always with a worn *chapan* draped over her head. The woman was always ushered into the family rooms, given a sweet table first and usually a full meal with a rice dish later. In other words, she was treated as an honored guest. Still, the women in the family did not visit her home. In the view of both parties, she was fulfilling an obligation through her visits. There was a prolonged greeting ritual conducted by the Kazakh woman, who asked about all male and female members of the family. If the man who got her son the job was present in the household, the Kazakh woman made a point of speaking to him personally.

Both Uzbeks and Tajiks were always included in the terms, *muhajir* and Ferghanachi. In tracing the kin connections for various families, there were no distinctions made between Uzbek and Tajik immigrants. Uzbek and Tajik families were linked within the same network. There was intermarriage on a fairly wide scale. Certainly, the rate of intermarriage between Ferghanachi Uzbeks and Tajiks was much higher than the corresponding intermarriage rate between *muhajir* Uzbeks and native Afghan Uzbeks, and *muhajir* Tajiks and native Tajiks. Nor were there any cultural differences between immigrant Uzbeks and Tajiks. Such symbolic items as the men's embroidered caps, women's dress, and foods were identical for both. The only difference was language use. A difference in the household language pattern in addition to knowledge of background and kin of families identified them as Uzbek or Tajik. Illustrating this was a conversation that occurred when an engagement was announced. A kinsman of a family was to be married and a Kasani neighborwoman asked one of the family who the bride was. The answer given was the girl's name, her parents' names, and, attached to the end, the explanation, Tajiki. The questioner understood from the answer that the family of the bride were *muhajir* Tajiks. The speaker would not have spoken of native Tajiks in this manner; a longer explanation would have been necessary. Tajik was thus the marked term in the pair of possibilities Uzbek/Tajik. If the bride's family had been *muhajir* Uzbeks, no explanatory term would have been given. Further, there was no town origin label given. The expression of linguistic criteria was felt more significant.

There were certain feelings that the Ferghana dialect of Uzbek was being lost. Some informants were unable to prevent the use of Persian even among their own children as that language gained reinforcement in the schools. Women were the primary carriers of Uzbek. They spoke it at all their gatherings. Younger men, on the other hand, were more likely to use Persian. In the 1970s there was a resurgent interest in Uzbek which was linked to various socio-political pressures emanating from Kabul.

Despite the attachment to Uzbek as part of the identity complex for most Ferghanachis, both languages had a great influence on each other. Interestingly, the Uzbek language spoken by the Ferghanachis was referred to as Uzbeki, with the Persian suffix indicating language. Informants were unfamiliar with the Turkic suffix, *cha*, which indicates language. Yet in Uzbekistan, the Uzbek language is known as Uzbekcha (Raun 1969:2). In Afghanistan, Persian had a continuing impact on Turkic linguistic practice; in Soviet Central Asia, the process was slowed down because of the standardization and written form of the Turkic languages.

In practice, linguistic criteria and the immigrant/native distinction were not wholly separated. The differing linguistic patterns of the homeland and Afghanistan influenced informants' judgments. An old Kasani once told me that in Afghanistan, no one was learning to speak properly. I asked him what he meant and he explained that Uzbek greetings always involve the formal form of the second person; the plural is used for addressing one individual. Thus, the greeting is: yakhshimi*siz*, jan*ingiz* jurmi, yakshi yurip*sizmi*. The use of the "siz" and "ingiz" forms indicates formality and politeness. Yet, the man complained, everyone in Afghanistan speaks like this and he spoke the typical Persian forms used in Afghanistan emphasizing the informal singular second person: Chetor as*ti*, khub as*ti*.[6] In his view, the speech, in fact, the overall behavior of the younger generations, was degenerating from the Afghan environment.

In this example, two distinct thoughts were linked together. The first was that Uzbek is a superior language spoken by a superior people who know the proper way to behave. The second was that Uzbek was somehow associated with Transoxania and Persian with Afghanistan, a view not quite correspondent to empirical reality. Despite the many Uzbek speakers native to Afghanistan, and the Persian speakers native to Transoxania, the attitude remained--Uzbek was the language of the homeland and Persian the language of exile. The old Kasani informant mentioned above was one of the few who spoke the Tajik dialect of Kasan. Yet he did not mourn the loss of this dialect the way he did the loss of Uzbek.

Ferghanachi identity then included several themes woven into a complex whole: Islam, ethnic endogamy and the Uzbek language. Rather than the lineal descent idiom used by other groups like the Pashtuns (Barth 1969: 19-20), the analogy between exile from Soviet Central Asia for religion's sake and Mohammed and his *muhajir* followers' flight from Mecca to Medina connected the group to the Islamic golden age. Emphasis on this factor led to the immigrant/native dichotomy discussed previously.

Proper Islamic behavior as viewed by the Ferghanachis kept brideprice down in order to facilitate close endogamous marriages. Marital endogamy and the resulting affinal links between families were as important to these people as lineal descent was to the Pashtuns. Moreover, intimacy within the household and between households at least partially cross-cutting the separation of the sexes was a direct result of the preferred pattern of endogamy.

Intermarriage with other ethnic groups was justified only by Islam, which thereby overshadowed even endogamy. The first interethnic wedding between a Ferghanachi girl and an outsider, a Persian-speaking man of the group known as Arab, occurred in 1977. Though there was much initial criticism of the marriage, Qari A. A., the girl's uncle and the moral authority of the community, remained steadfast in his view that all that mattered was that the groom was a good Muslim (Shalinsky 1980). The groom was an orphan and the Quranic rules about care for widows and orphans were invoked in favor of the marriage.

The final portion of the identity complex was the significance attributed to the Uzbek language. There was widespread feeling that Uzbek was the language of the lost homeland, of proper speech, while Persian was the language of Afghanistan and assimilation.

## NOTES

1. See also "Islam and Ethnicity: The Northern Afghanistan Perspective." Central Asian Survey 1(2):41-85.

2. This example comes from the 1977 fieldwork of Whitney Azoy (personal communication) who worked on *buzkashi* in the Kunduz region.

3. Turkestan was not usually called the *watan*, homeland. Sometimes Tajikistan was used to mean all Soviet Central Asia (Slobin 1976:9). That the *watan* was Shurawi and Tajikistan was another clue that these emigrants were accustomed to Soviet usage, that they emigrated during the Soviet period.

4. In the case of interethnic marriage, the family involved often had severed its contacts from the group or had behaved in ways considered inappropriate by the *qawm*. Typical was the case of a Bukharai teacher in the girl's school married to an Afghan Uzbek. She had been permitted to continue her education, thereby creating a scandal.

5. The joke was on the villager and reinforced the stereotype that Uzbeks are dumb. See Chapter 1 for Schuyler's story of Shirin and Ferhat.

6. The Kasanis used the second person plural in Persian sometimes, thus *chetor asten, khub asten*, spoken with the second vowel similar to short a. This pattern may date from the Tajik dialect of the Ferghana Valley, coincident with the Uzbek pattern.

# Part III

Refugees Again

# Chapter 7

## Afghanistan from 1978-1990

The coup of April 27, 1978 was organized by a coalition of Marxist-oriented groups including the Khalq (People's) and Parcham (flag or banner) parties. The Khalq party emerged victorious from early factional struggles and eliminated its opponents from the government. Though the leadership in Khalq was strongly Pashtun, early in the regime President Taraki announced a new program for the ethnic minorities based on the Soviet nationalities policy model. The minorities were to be part of the government, training in the minority languages was to begin in the schools and newspapers were to be published in certain minority languages including Uzbek. The lack of early resistance to the government has been attributed in part to the new ethnic policy but the general consensus now seems to be that the playing of the ethnic card was not completely successful (Newman 1988; Naby 1988a:66-68 and 1988b).

One Kunduz Ferghanachi did become active on *Yulduz,* the new officially organized Uzbek weekly newspaper, which first appeared in July 1978. However, informants stressed that they were familiar with and opposed to Khalq policy and ideology from the moment that they came to power. Early opposition emanated from the local religious authorities through the network of mosques.

After Sayid Harun, who might have become an important religious authority for the Afghan-born generation, was killed by the regime in 1978 (as discussed later in this chapter,) the Ferghanachis of Kunduz began to prepare to leave the country or, at the very least, to move to Kabul, from which it was easier to leave. They also began to support the resistance with money, clothing and food.

The Soviet invasion of December 1979 was especially horrifying to people who had left their homes only fifty years before to escape the Soviet transformation of their society (Edwards 1987:48). From many locations in northern Afghanistan, the air invasion force could be seen. Soviet tanks passed through major cities on their way to combat. Airports were used as Soviet military bases. Since many at this point were not optimistic about the resistance's chance for success against the Soviets, plans to leave Afghanistan accelerated.

Many of the households of the two Ferghanachi *mahallas* were taken over by local party officials. Before leaving Kunduz, the owners frequently made *giraw* contracts with parties who were staying. These contracts involved an arrangement in which one party, the lender, paid a sum for residence rights for an unspecified time period to another leaving the country who retained ownership rights. The owner promised to repay the exact amount upon his return, and if he did not, the property became the lender's. While such contracts were binding when made through the government court system, most people arranged these privately and thus the government, which viewed this as illegal abandonment of property by counter-revolutionaries, confiscated the property.

In rural areas, resistance to the Afghan regime by both Uzbeks and Tajiks was extremely strong. In the countryside around Kunduz, the situation was worse than in the city through the mid-1980s. The choice of remaining in the villages to fight was widely made until 1984 when the Soviets advanced a policy of complete destruction (Naby 1988a:65). Helsinki Watch and Asia Watch, two human rights organizations based in the United States, have reported that one of the largest massacres in Afghanistan occurred in Kunduz province.[1] They have independent accounts of the massacre which include direct testimony from survivors. In mid-December of 1984, Soviet forces looted houses, destroyed food, burned crops, raped women and killed a number of villagers in Chahar Darra district. In retaliation, the resistance attacked the Soviet column on its way back to the city. Apparently in reprisal for this attack, which inflicted only minor damage, Soviet troops and a few party members went to the village of Haji Rahmatullah on December 22 and systematically executed all the inhabitants they found, including women and children. They then set fire to the houses. When the resistance forces entered the area afterward they discovered,

> Every family's members were shot along with their small children while sitting by the heaters inside the rooms. Most of them were killed while still in sitting positions around their fireplaces. We saw many of the ladies holding their babies tight in their bosoms, both being shot together. In most of the cases many people were brought into one house and then the place was hand grenaded and fired [burned]. . . (Laber and Rubin 1988:26).

The number of dead was estimated at 250. Survivors and some of the *mujahidin* in the area took the bodies of the murdered women and children (reports differ on which bodies), loaded them onto carts and took them to Kunduz city to the governor as a protest.

> On the way to Kunduz the people received us in every village with eyes full of tears. When the procession approached Kunduz city, the governor received the procession outside the city. The aged men and women of the region who had accompanied the procession could not control their sentiments on seeing the governor and started cursing him and calling, "Shame to you and your criminals. . . . (testimony of Mohammed Jan quoted in Laber and Rubin:26)

. . . And the governor didn't care about the dead bodies, and he said, take
your dead bodies away, I can't do anything about it. The Afghan military
officers, the other people working with the government, KHAD [the secret
police], government servants, they told us, "It was not our work, it is the
Russians who are committing all these cruelties and we don't have any
power or right to do anything. . . (testimony of Mohammed Taher quoted
in Laber and Rubin:27)

One of the people interviewed about this massacre noted that the *mujahidin* of this
area had attacked the Soviets many times and had even captured and killed a
Russian general some months before this event. The Soviets had therefore acted in
retaliation for his death. This is also reported in Gall (1988:212-214). I was told
the story of this massacre and the people's procession with the corpses on the carts
by an informant in 1985. He also attributed the Soviet response to the killing of a
Russian general by the *mujahidin*.

The countryside around Kunduz, especially near Chahar Darra and Khanabad,
continued to be a major Soviet target in 1985 with reports of village bombings,
children killed by cutting their throats and setting them on fire with petrol. Women
and children were the targets since men were not usually in the villages when the
Soviets would arrive but were with the *mujahidin* (Laber and Rubin 1988:28, 37,
55). Other reports mention the deliberate destruction of the harvest, crop storage
areas and irrigation canals in the province (Laber and Rubin 1988: 59-60, 63; Gall
1988:201). Some of this may have been a deliberate policy of terror (Lemercier-
Quelquejay and Bennigsen 1984:208).

In August 1988 after the Soviets had withdrawn half of their forces according
to the negotiated withdrawal, the resistance captured the city of Kunduz.
Apparently, the *mujahidin* were able to enter the city after the Soviet forces had
evacuated. Planes flying from Soviet territory then bombed the city, forcing the
resistance to withdraw so that the Afghan government forces could regain control.
The bombing was a major violation of the negotiated withdrawal agreement.
Informants in Pakistan reported that the bombings destroyed much of the center of
the city including the area where the Ferghanachis had owned the *chapan* selling
shops.

### Ideological Commitments of the Feghanachis

To understand how the Ferghanachis interpreted Afghanistan's political turmoil
between 1978 and today, their attitudes toward the resistance's fight against the
Marxist government, and their political role and participation in the future of
Afghanistan, we must examine the new generation of leaders, the generation of

Afghanistan-born men now generally in their forties but whose formative years were in the 1950s-1960s. These men have confronted modernity, rapid change, and the major ideological currents of Marxism and Islamism in their lifetimes. Their common experiences and decisions may tell us about the future of their community.

Under Prime Minister Daoud, the 1950s were crucial for the development of the Afghan nation-state. In a series of five-year plans, education was made available for the first time to provincial youth including non-Pashtuns. Secularism, especially in urban areas, and the penetration of the capitalist market economy continued to increase as did the governmental bureaucracy. The 1960s brought an experiment in democracy with the new constitution of 1964. Many of the newly educated young people began to participate in politics for the first time. Kabul University became the scene for confrontations between those students espousing various forms of communism and their opponents who organized a Muslim Youth group along Islamist lines inspired by the Muslim Brothers in Egypt.[2] Both the leftists and the Islamist students agreed that the Musahiban dynasty was corrupt and should be replaced through revolutionary action.

Traditional political loyalties based on tribe, ethnic group and sect were not replaced in these ideological struggles. Rather the old politics were augmented by the new ideologies which questioned the legitimacy of the state because of current injustices based on class analysis or Quranic principles. The situation deteriorated after Daoud's 1973 coup against the King, his cousin. While tolerating the communists because of some initial support, Daoud suppressed and persecuted the Muslim Youth organization, forcing some into exile in Pakistan. He also reemphasized Pashtun ethnic dominance by abolishing a few of the rights other minorities had gained including radio broadcasts in the Turkic languages (Shahrani 1986: 58-65; Aziz 1987:60). It was during the 1960s in time to witness the confrontations between leftist and Islamist ideologies that the young Afghan-born Ferghanachi men first gained political consciousness. Men of the first Afghan-born generation illustrate the search for ways to blend the old ethnic loyalties, Islam, scientific and technological advance, and politics.

### Sayid Harun Shahid (the martyr)

The first martyr from the Kasani *mahalla* in Kunduz was 35-year-old Sayid Harun, son of Qari A. A., killed in 1978 during the Taraki regime. In his memory and honor, Sayid Harun's name was taken by the organizers of the Ferghanachi *mujahidin* as the name for their resistance group which still operates in the Kunduz-Baghlan region.

In an interview during the fall of 1976, Sayid Harun discussed several topics which illustrate the views of his generation. At the time of the interview, the fact that an American woman anthropologist had begun to study the community was a matter of some controversy. Early one morning Sayid Harun, who was working and residing in Baghlan at this time, sent for the anthropologist to come to his father's house. I had no idea who he was, but the people at whose household I was staying insisted that I go immediately. Sayid Harun spoke to me alone, in itself an unusual circumstance, which illustrates his own moral certainty and also the possibility that no one else was permitted to be there. He offered his help and his willingness to answer any questions I might have. Perhaps his purpose was to support M. (see below) who was one of his best friends; they had attended Kabul University together.

In the interview Sayid Harun spoke primarily of the significance of Islam in peoples' daily lives. He emphasized the inner communion with God that ought to occur during prayer. He said, "The presence of others in the room ought to be irrelevant to the one praying. A person even aware of others during prayer is not properly experiencing devotion to God." When asked about the role of Naqshbandi sufism in the current Kasani *mahalla,* he said he believed that this had been more significant in the past in the Ferghana Valley homeland where his father and others of the emigrant generation had been directly involved in Naqshbandi orders. He also spoke of the need to educate people in true Islam so that they no longer believed in such things as capturing jinns in bottles for curing. As shown in this summary of his conversation, his attitudes demonstrate the influence of a progressive Islamic education with strong ties to traditional *ulema* (Muslim scholars) of whom his father was a notable example.[3]

Sayid Harun asked me if I was being pressured to become Muslim. Unlike many in the community who pressed the issue out of sincere conviction and friendship, he urged me to maintain my own beliefs. He said that when one is surrounded by people far from family and home, one is too easily influenced. He himself had studied in India and had apparently been exposed to ideas and situations very different from his upbringing. Again his view here is not what we in the West would consider to be typical of an Islamic "fundamentalist." Yet unquestionably at Kabul University in the late 1960s, his political sympathy and ideology were with the Muslim Youth Organization (Shalinsky 1984:53; Shahrani 1984). As the son of one of the highest religious authorities in the neighborhood, it was expected that Sayid Harun would gradually grow into and take over his father's role as a mosque leader and community elder. During the summer of 1978 while serving as a mosque official in the Kunduz neighborhood, he gave many sermons which included allusions to anti-government themes using passages from the Quran.

Having been at the University in the late 1960s, Sayid Harun was quite familiar with the fact that the new government was communist just as he was familiar with the remnants of the Muslim Youth Organization in exile in Pakistan.

According to informants, at the Friday prayer when there was a large audience including many outsiders, he spoke in veiled allusions. When only the Ferghanachis were present, he spoke openly. The precipitating cause of his arrest by the regime is not known, but some believe the governor of the province, a Khalq party member, heard and recorded one or more of the Friday sermons on a cassette recorder. Harun was imprisoned for two months, then taken out to a desolate region in the countryside with 35 others and executed.

The family was not notified of his death immediately but was told that all the prisoners had been transferred to Kabul. The day before the execution, an acquaintance of Sayid Harun came to his uncle and offered to get him released for 200,000 afghanis before he was shot. The man said he could bribe the Khalq official in charge of the executions. The uncle considered this man a cheat and did not believe that his nephew was in such imminent danger. No bribe was made. The death of Sayid Harun was not confirmed until Hafizullah Amin, who seized power from Taraki, published lists of people who had been executed by the prior regime. Further confirmation came when Babrak Karmal and the Parcham party came into power. The local Khalq official in charge of execution was arrested and found to have millions of afghanis of bribe money in his possession. (Shalinsky 1984a:53-54).

The martyrdom of Sayid Harun galvanized the community who began to consider making *hijrat*. Sayid Harun's father is now in Saudi Arabia where many other Ferghanachis now live. He teaches the Quran. Sayid Harun's son born in 1977 is also now a *qari*; he resides in his grandfather's household.

### M. the Teacher

M., the oldest son of Haji Omar the bootmaker *(see Chapter 3)*, was a high school English teacher at the boy's school. He had graduated from high school in Kunduz, passed the university entrance exam and attended Kabul University. By 1976 he had been teaching in Kunduz for five years and, within the next few years as the head of the English department, he set the English curriculum and testing for the region. Fluent in Dari (Afghan Persian), Uzbek, Pashto and English, he was one of a very few individuals from outside Kabul who worked part-time teaching Dari to Peace Corps volunteers.

As a university student at the same time as Sayid Harun, M. was also exposed to the same ideological currents and conflicts concerning the solution of social problems, tradition, modernity and Islam. Contacts with outsiders in Kabul including many Americans created problems with colleagues because his occupation, high school teaching, was dominated by members of other ethnic groups, many with leftist or communist leanings. Both his experiences in Kabul and as a Kunduz teacher were acutely contradictory to the more traditional lifestyle of his family, kin network and neighborhood. M.'s identity was constructed on two premises, Uzbek nationalism and Islam, the former perhaps dominant before the Afghan revolution and the latter becoming increasingly significant during the communist regime.

M. took his Uzbek identity from his mother who was from the Kokand region and who did not speak any Persian when she came to Afghanistan. Early in his school days, he took an Uzbek pen-name, a militant affirmation of the Uzbek identity. During his childhood, his family was among the poorest in the *mahalla* and eventually his father's bootmaking shop went bankrupt. After his return from the university, he was the financial support of the family, allowing his younger sister and brother to marry and his parents to make the pilgrimage to Mecca. M. was drawn to the greater financial opportunities available to him in Kabul. This was a source of tension between him and his father.

M. decided to take me into his household because he thought it would be an interesting experience. He took the traditional animosity toward the Russians who had taken the Central Asian homeland one step further by actually liking and interacting with Americans to the greatest extent possible. Some years earlier, he had gone so far as to have a traditional dinner in the household guesthouse for the visiting American Ambassador without getting permission from the Afghan government. He did not ask the community elders for permission regarding my stay because "they would never have agreed." He informed them I was arriving. He also ignored the advice of many of his closest friends and relatives. What intrigued him about my study? When we met, I expressed interest in his family background; I asked questions about the Uzbek language; I knew about the history of Central Asia including stories about Enver Pasha and the Basmachis. These topics were important to him.

M. had participated in a study group whose members had promised to speak only in Uzbek. He always wore the cap worn by those in Uzbekistan rather than the Ferghanachi embroidered cap. He preferred classical Central Asian music which could occasionally be picked up on the radio from Dushanbe, the capital of Tajikistan, to the music on radio Kabul. He spoke Uzbek in the bazaar with Turkmens, Afghan Uzbeks, Kazakhs, and *muhajir* Uzbeks, and would even speak it in school to the appropriate students to make a point about linguistic discrimination. Though he would speak Pashto to Pashtuns in the bazaar "to get the price down," he would also avow his identity as an Uzbek when questioned by Pashtuns.

M. prayed five times daily, attended mosque regularly, fasted during Ramadan and did not drink alcohol though undoubtedly in Kabul he had the opportunity. His views on Islam were similar to Sayid Harun's. For example, they both affirmed the existence of the *jinn*, beings created of smokeless fire, since such beings are mentioned in the Quran. However, they did not believe the popular folk elaborations of these beliefs. The Kasani religious leader, Mawlewi Abdur Rahman once said that M. was a good boy though he did frequently tell him to get his hair cut and also to shave his mustache, which was generally viewed by the community as a Kabuli or Pashtun custom.

After the April Revolution, M.'s working environment created difficulties for him. A new principal came and teachers were strongly "encouraged" to join the communist party. M.'s political inclinations were well known in Kunduz and he feared that he would be arrested. The growth of a beard indicated his sympathies with the Islamist parties. The situation became tenser and he decided to leave for Pakistan via the southern part of the country. When a travelling companion was arrested near the border, M. found that one of the young soldiers making arrests was a former student. He could have abandoned his companion and left because his former student would have allowed it but he chose to stay and go to prison. He believes that because he was arrested far from Kunduz, he was not badly treated. He served eight months and never again returned to Kunduz.

He described his time in prison. "Islam was everything to us. Every day we read and studied the Quran. That's all." After his release, M. went to Kabul where he was involved in helping people arrange passage to Pakistan. In 1983 he and his four oldest children escaped to Pakistan while his wife and two youngest children took a more circuitous route through Saudi Arabia. Having many American acquaintances influenced his decision to apply to come to the United States as a political refugee. His decision was predicated on the hope that his children would have the opportunity for a good education and a good future in the United States. Living in a western university town initially, M. and his family quickly became leaders in the local Muslim community. As a Persian speaker and as a Sunni, M. found that he became a mediator in local disputes between Iranians and other Muslims. For some time, he served as imam and gave the Friday public sermons. In 1985 he and his family moved to the east coast where they could be closer to kin and fellow ethnics. Throughout his time in the United States, M. was involved with supporting the cause of the Ferghanachi *mujahid* group which is affiliated with Hizb-i Islami (Gulbuddin Hekmatyar's party).

## A. the Skeptic

In the same Kunduz neighborhood as the fathers of Sayid Harun and M., another emigrant from Kasan, A. H. had raised three sons to adulthood. At the time of my fieldwork, the oldest son was a principal in Mazar-i Sharif, the youngest son was studying engineering in Tashkent and the middle son, A., was the owner of a radio repair shop in the Kunduz bazaar. A. and M. were married to sisters. A. was the same age as Sayid Harun.

A. was a firm believer in technological progress and modernization. He was apparently less committed to Islamic observance than were most of the community and he was known for his leftist political sympathies. He could also eat three huge platters of rice *pilaw* at one meal.

One of our early encounters occurred because the provincial governor had sent a policeman to check on me, upsetting Haji Omar in whose household I was staying. I had been attending a women's gathering at the time, was thus unavailable, and then returned to find an uproar in which it was not clear who had come and for what reason. When I spoke about this to A. later that day, he said not to worry or do anything and that he would take care of it. There was never any similar incident though A.'s sister said that the governor wanted to move me and have me stay with them.

This was the time of Daoud (1976) and A. must have had some sort of political connections although it is difficult to surmise precisely what they were. Unusual for an Uzbek and *muhajir*, A. had been a career army officer. Though he had supported Daoud's coup against the king in July 1973, he was accused by a superior officer of dereliction of duty because of anti-Daoud sentiments. Many local people believed ethnic discrimination was at the root of this charge. A. spent several years in prison and after his release, opened the radio repair shop.

A. openly denigrated what he viewed as some of the more questionable aspects of Islam. For example, he repeatedly denied the existence of jinn or any sort of supernatural creatures. Others who heard him say these sorts of things would argue with him, remonstrate in fear and generally try to explain to me that he was just joking. A. also would joke with me that we should go to the bar at the Intercontinental Hotel in Kabul. Once he asked to hide liquor in my trunks.

A. was most interested in western technology and technological achievement. He very much wanted my mini cassette recorder as a gift. He also looked forward with much anticipation to a trip to the Soviet Union to visit his brother.[4] He hoped to obtain items to help in his business. His mother begged me to try to persuade him not to go. She and others in the community believed that visiting the Soviet Union was a sin. It was the homeland lost to the unbelievers. After a person makes *hijrat* and finds a place of refuge, he should not return except for *jihad* unless a legitimate governmental authority comes to power. A. could not be persuaded against the trip.

The news of A.'s murder came in August of 1977 in an aerogram. "A. . . . as you know wanted to go to Russia. Finally he did and after 48 days we got a news that he was killed in Tashkent in Gh.'s [his brother's] room in the dormitory. His body came in the same day. We buried him on July 26th in Kunduz. That was the worst happening that ever happened in our *mahalla*. His death made everybody here sad and made the life of his family very difficult. . . . The reason of the murder is not known to us." In early November in another letter, the incident was mentioned. "In the early days everyone went crazy. Still no accurate news . . . Some news came and they say it was a thief that killed him but we don't believe it." The murder of A. in the land of the unbelievers under suspicious circumstances reinforced the prevailing view that Central Asia under the Soviets continued to be a bad place despite its technological superiority to Afghanistan. Furthermore, the death of A. took place only eight months before the Marxist coup in Afghanistan, again adding to the suspicious nature of the event as people considered it in retrospect.

A.'s widow and several of his children are now in Karachi, Pakistan. They left Afghanistan during the summer of 1989 having lived for much of the time after the revolution with relatives in Kabul. Since the death occurred in the Soviet Union in *dar al harb* (the land in which there is on-going *jihad* since the time of the *hijrat* of the community), there has been some reinterpretation of the events, perhaps for the sake of the widow and children in the context of the current *jihad*. A.'s youngest son was only three when his father died and he does not remember him. Like many boys his age, he is ready to go and participate in the *jihad* and become *shahid*, a martyr. The boy sometimes asked his grandmother whether his father was *shahid*. She answered in the affirmative and they used the title when writing letters to the neighborhood school operated by the *mujahidin*. I asked someone else outside of the Karachi community whether A., whose leftist political and anti-religious views were well known, could be considered to be *shahid* and he said no. This person said that A. was killed by a Soviet Uzbek and not a Russian. Though people are called *shahid* of a lesser degree even when there is no *jihad* in the case of accidental death or death in childbirth, he did not think the murder of A. warranted this title of honor.

There are many other men born in Afghanistan to parents who left the Ferghana Valley who share certain characteristic attitudes with the men detailed here. The public relations representative of Hizb-i Islami [Hekmatyar's group] in the United States is of this background although he is from Kabul. On one notable occasion in the Washington, D.C. area, Soviet Uzbek entertainers, who were visiting the United States and performing as part of a folk arts celebration at the Smithsonian, were invited to a Ferghanachi engagement party. The Hizb representative led the celebrants, including the Soviet Uzbeks, in prayer for the victory of the *mujahidin* in Afghanistan. He embraced the Soviet Uzbeks at the end of the prayer.

In these portraits, several common threads are particularly significant for understanding the Ferghanachis' point of view regarding events surrounding the Marxist coup in Afghanistan and the subsequent resistance. The portraits clearly show that the Ferghanachis were not aloof from the national culture of Afghanistan nor were they engaged in a protracted struggle against the central government's authority, an explanation frequently used by western writers to explain the resistance to the Marxist government. If anything, the lives of these men indicate that involvement in national institutions, especially education and even the military, were seen as paths to individual and community advancement. Though the community had reason to distrust the government for its pro-Pashtun policies and its lack of support in the struggle against the Russo/Soviets in Central Asia, the resentment was superceded by desire for new opportunities as well as greater participation in the national culture and national institutions but their hopes and expectations were not fulfilled by the Musahiban dynasty.

Also apparent in the three cases are the choices which the men made in the problematic arena of what might be termed progressive Islam versus secularism (Canfield 1985:63). It is striking that with the exception of A. and a few others, the Afghan-born generation of the Ferghanachis have aligned themselves with the Islamic Revolutionary parties. Of particular note is the strong involvement with Hekmatyar's party and its supplying of the Sayid Harun Shahid guerrilla band. Western sources have indicated that Hekmatyar's Hizb-i Islami is primarily composed of detribalized, that is, urbanized Pashtuns.[5] In fact, Chaliand (1985: 55) compares them to those who were attracted to the Khalq party, one of the Communist groups, in that modest middle class teachers and low-ranking bureaucrats are typical members. While not all Ferghanachis would take the position that Hekmatyar is to be trusted not to reinstitute Pashtun dominance, that some do trust him is testimony to the integrative power of resurgent Islam.[6]

Islam potentially provides a means by which newly educated people from diverse ethnolinguistic backgrounds can be formed into a new unified community (Naby 1986a:125 1986b:298). This Islam, whether it be called revolutionary, revivalist, or reformist, is a modern movement based on concepts such as political party, which had their origins in the West. This Islam is based on a return to basic texts, the Quran and hadith, but there is also the call for social reform, spiritual revitalization, and radical transformation of society (Canfield: 1989:29). In the Ferghanachi alliance to Hizb may also be the beginning of class allegiances replacing former ethnic and tribal loyalties (Farr 1987:128). Once again, the affiliation with Hizb and other Islamist parties is not a backward step as it is often perceived by outside commentators. For the Ferghanachis, it is another sign of their integration into the national culture, participation with other ethnic and possibly similar class groups. As such the choice of A. and others for secularism is but the other side of the same coin. Advanced technology and its associated scientific ideology or a leftist political orientation provides a similar attempt at the integration of disparate economic interests and social forces as well as a similar utopian ideal. Because of the history of the Ferghanachis as *muhajirs* from Central Asia, the Islamic ideology is a more logical choice for the majority of the community.

The commitment to Islam as a unifying force is especially clear in the martyrdom book devoted to the late commander of the Sayid Harun guerilla group which was among the treasured mementos of many households in Pakistan in 1989-1990. The commander, killed in 1988, had a background similar to the men already described. The rhetoric of martyrdom is apparent in the following selection devoted to his memory.

## *The Book of Martyrs*

**For the memory of the martyr, the bloody-shrouded Mawlewi Abdul Fattah 'Adili, commandant of Sayid Harun Shahid group.**

**Here again another star has arrived in the skies of martyrdom. Another great man who truly wanted to give his life for Islam began to walk into the path of martyrdom knowingly; and he joined history. Our brother *mujahid*, Mawlewi Abdul Fattah 'Adili, the commandant of Imam Bukhari base and also Sayid Harun Shahid group's commandant, who was truly a symbol of the concept of *mujahid*, had fought until his last breath of life, lived like a *mujahid*, and became a martyr like the *mujahids* at the beginning of Islam.**

**This spiritual fighter came into this world thirty-nine years ago in a religious family in Kunduz. His father Mawlewi 'Adil always sought to give his son the best Islamic education. Shahid 'Adili joined religious study at Madrassah Khiyaban[7] according to his father's wish and received his religious knowledge from scholars such as Mawlewi Taj Muhammad and Mawlewi Abdul Nasir. In 1348 (1969) he joined the Madrassah Takharistan[8] and after graduating became a teacher there. While studying, he was actively involved in Islamic demonstrations and activities and deliberately joined the Muslim Youth in 1350 (1971). Brother Abdul Fattah played a key**

role in Kunduz province by giving a pure Islamic education to the youth. After the communist coup in Afghanistan, he accelerated his secret activities and organized the groups engaging in armed struggle in the city of Kunduz.

In 1359 (1980), he was arrested by the Russian puppets [local Marxist government officials], but by the mercy of God, our brother was able to successfully escape the regime's jail[9] and made *hijrat* to Pakistan. Brother Mawlewi Abdul Fattah 'Adili and a group of other brothers, while in *hijrat*, struggled to establish a military group in Kunduz and adjacent provinces. They organized a group of young fighters in 1361 (1982) under Hizb-i Islami [Gulbuddin Hekmatyar's party] by the name of Sayid Harun Shahid's group. They joined other righteous groups who were fighting against evil.

Because of his and others' unceasing struggle, they were able to establish a homebase which became one the strongest fortresses against the unbelievers. Under the leadership of Brother Abdul Fattah 'Adili, the *mujahidin* in Sayid Harun Shahid's group, shoulder to shoulder with other *mujahidin*, participated in countless operations with amazing success. Finally, Brother Abdul Fattah 'Adili, on 10-27-1367 (1988) in an operation done by Hizb-i Islami to crush the unbelievers and conquer the city and airport of Kunduz, was martyred and joined the mercy of God.

> No doubt we are from God and we will return to Him. (Sura I:155).

> May his soul be happy. May his name be respected. May his spirit be everlasting.

One of the special characteristics of this spiritual struggler was that he was an open-minded *mujahid* who considered his main responsibility the creation of unity of the Islamic parties and all the Islamic forces committed to an Islamic Revolution. Naturally, his activities opened the hearts of the common people. As a result the hearts of the *mujahidin* and the people of the region were full of love for this spiritual struggler. The bloody history of our country will witness that Shahid 'Adili will be honored by all the people who raise the green flag of Islamic struggle with hearts unmarred by arrogance and whose bloody fight is continuing. All the *mujahidin* and the fighters in Sayid Harun Shahid's group, in addition to congratulating this spiritual struggler's honored martyrdom, once again promise God to continue his path until a legitimate Islamic government comes into being in Afghanistan.

> In memory of 'Adili the Hero [a poem translated in prose form]
> He participated and was in the front lines in any battle. He had a high position in his bloody shroud. He became martyred on the battlefield while he stood and attacked. He followed the straight path in his *jihad* and struggle according to the teaching of the *Shariat* and Quran. In the trenches

he was like a lion because of his bravery and belief. The enemies were crushed by his orders and attacks. Everyone admired his convictions and commitment to *jihad.* His wisdom played a key role in his battle plan. Finally, he drank the cup of martyrdom because of pure love. In doing so, he decorated Islamic history once again. His martyrdom and his belief are the pride of his generation. All his friends and followers in the trenches are waiting to join him. Tulips will grow in the homeland from each drop of his blood. All the nation is indebted because of his honesty and fidelity. No eye fails to shed tears upon hearing his name. His visage is inscribed in God's design. May his name live forever. The nation blesses his pure spirit. May all his fellows be saved by God. Makhdum [the author] says may God crown his head with honor.

In comparing the biographical information on this commander to the men described above, similar themes are again apparent. The commander attended the government *madrassah* in Kunduz and became a teacher there, indicating involvement in government institutions and commitment to participation in the national culture. During the early 1970s, approximately the same time or shortly after Sayid Harun was at Kabul University, Shahid 'Adili joined the Muslim Youth organization, again the choice of the Islamist ideology at the time when it was competing against Marxism for the allegiances of students and teachers. The emphasis on the commander's role in fostering unity among the various Islamist groups is also significant in reinforcing the theme that Islam itself is ideally perceived as the major force in the creation of political unity and further, that a state based upon Islam would therefore engender the kind of unity and social justice that the Musahiban state lacked.

## NOTES

1. An exception to the omission of these accounts of massacres in the western press is Klass 1985:28-29.

2. Progressive Islam had several different forms including revolutionism (Canfield 1985:65).

3. Sayid Harun and his father, even more so, embody the three most important qualities needed for religious authority among Sunnis in Afghanistan: knowledge of Islamic jurisprudence and theology, spiritual power attained through apprenticeship in a Sufi order, and descent from a noble ancestor (Canfield 1985:60).

4. Olivier Roy (1985:136) believes that because traditional social structures had disappeared among the Uzbeks, they were fascinated by modernity and technological advance. He attributes the lack of Uzbek involvement in the Afghan resistance to this. Although this example fits Roy's

perspective, most of my informants say that the leftist position was a minority one among Uzbeks and they dispute the interpretation that Uzbeks were not involved in the resistance movement.

5.  According to Canfield (1985:70), David Edwards has commented on Hekmatyar's ethnic base among Pashtuns emphasizing the anti-Sufi and anti-superstition ideology and that they are very weak at the grassroots level. This last point seems debatable.

6.  Even in the wake of conflict between Hekmatyar's and other *mujahid* forces in Kabul in 1992, some Ferghanachis militantly continue their support of Hizb. Others feel that their doubts regarding Hekmatyar's Pashtun chauvinism have been confirmed and they strongly oppose him.

7.  This *madrassah* was located in the larger of the two Ferghanachi *mahallas* in Kunduz.

8.  This was the state-run *madrassah* in Kunduz.

9.  An informant said that he was actually in the offices of KHAD, the secret police, but when he was alone, he broke a window and fled the city before he could be transferred to prison.

# Chapter 8

# Pakistan

Data on the current location of members from the core Ferghanachi households of *mahalla* Kasani indicates that at least portions of two-thirds of the households have migrated to Saudi Arabia. However, over 25 percent of the core households have members who remain in Kunduz in their original location. Some of these are women and children. The remainder of the households or portions of them are divided among internal migration to Kabul and external to Pakistan, Turkey, and the United States. The high percentage of people already in Saudi Arabia, from over two-thirds of the households in the original Kunduz sample, and the relatively low number of Ferghanachis in Pakistan, perhaps only members of one hundred households from all over Afghanistan, indicates that the out-migration process is probably nearly complete.

Analysis of the movement of people out of Afghanistan into Pakistan and beyond indicates that the community has divided itself into two overlapping groups who are viewed as distinct. One group consists of those who view the stay in Pakistan or elsewhere as a transient state which is merely a preparation for the return to Afghanistan when a new legitimate government is able to take power there. These are the people who view themselves yet once again as *muhajirs* for they have sought a place of safe refuge enabling some to go back and participate in the *jihad*. The *muhajir* status has power and value in Islamic discourse. It incorporates a claim to protection and yet a refusal to become a "naturalized" citizen wherever one has relocated (Malkki 1992:35). It is commonly held that most Afghans in the refugee camps will return to Afghanistan and thus they would also appropriately be called *muhajirs*. Since the Ferghanachis who are *muhajirs* frequently do not go to the refugee camps, including the camp near Karachi, their identity is self-imposed. One informant stated that the Ferghanachis are reluctant to go to the refugee camps because they are urban and do not want to live in tents. Unlike the Ferghanachis, those in the camps have no other choice but to return to Afghanistan some day because international recognition and aid depend on the assumption that some day all people in the camps will return.

Some Ferghanachis do not seek to return to Afghanistan. They see Pakistan as yet another way station on a continuing journey which may end in other locations such as Saudi Arabia. These people are more displaced, more rootless, more liminal; they refer to themselves as the travellers, the *musafirs*. It is the same word as that used for people making ordinary train or plane trips and travelling from one place to another. Informants stated that this identity label is accurate because people know they are going to Saudi Arabia or Turkey sometime though they are not sure when. Informants compared themselves unfavorably to the previous generation who came from Turkestan and likewise ignored their own participation in the institutions and national culture of Afghanistan. "Unlike the generation who came from Uzbekistan, we, our children and our children's children are less attached to a homeland. The ones who came into Afghanistan were the true *muhajirs* because they would have returned to Turkestan at any time." Feelings of rootlessness and loss are expressed in these remarks.

The Ferghanachis typically do not stay in Peshawar or Quetta after arrival in Pakistan. Rather they move to Karachi, a pattern which has been established since the first wave of migration before 1981 *(Map 8.1)*. At that time many were advised by relatives in Saudi Arabia, where there was a long-established Ferghanachi community, to go to Karachi which had been used as a major transit point for people making the *haj*. According to informants, in the early period of the migration, it was easier to get forged identification and passports in Karachi than in Peshawar or elsewhere for leaving Pakistan. The pattern then established has continued to the present. Thus in certain parts of Karachi, one finds both Ferghanachis who are *muhajirs* and ones who are *musafirs*. Some cannot decide which they are and some, even when they have made a choice, hold to the other alternative as a future possibility.

One informant estimated that around 80 percent of the Ferghanachis go to Saudi Arabia with much smaller numbers going to Turkey, the United States, or other European countries. He believed that the majority are not interested either in remaining in Pakistan long term or in returning to Afghanistan and they live where they do because they are able to obtain financial support from their relatives already abroad. Because relatives send money or they are able to bring out some capital, the Ferghanachis are eventually able to set up small stores in the bazaar area of their urban neighborhoods. Thus, they form part of the estimated 600,000+ unregistered refugee population in Pakistan (Boesen 1988:226).

Members of other ethnic groups themselves recognize this as a pattern. In Peshawar, while accompanying another anthropologist in the area called the Afghan colony, we spoke with a jeweler from Badakhshan. When my study was explained to him, he said, "I know of those people; they always go to Karachi and then to Saudi Arabia."

Unlike most Afghans who remain in Pakistan, many Ferghanachis in Saudi Arabia will probably never return to Afghanistan. Having experienced the loss of two homelands in this century, they may well be too discouraged to go back and rebuild once again. At the least, one informant estimated, ninety percent of the people in Saudi Arabia will not return to Afghanistan even if a legitimate Islamic government takes power. Though the majority of Ferghanachis are *musafirs*, some

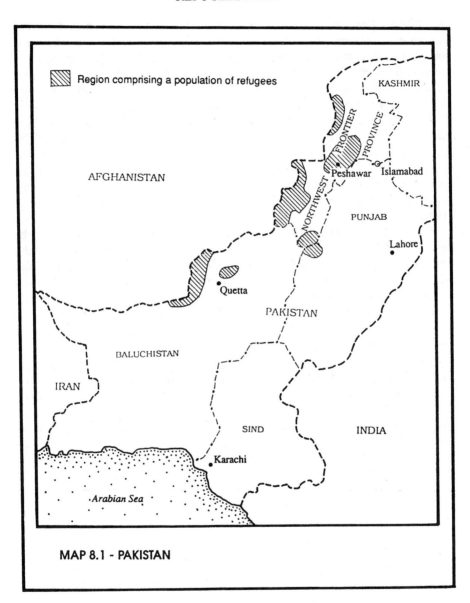

Region comprising a population of refugees

KASHMIR

AFGHANISTAN

NORTHWEST FRONTIER PROVINCE

Peshawar  Islamabad

PUNJAB

Lahore

Quetta

PAKISTAN

BALUCHISTAN

IRAN

SIND

INDIA

Karachi

*Arabian Sea*

**MAP 8.1 - PAKISTAN**

are waiting in Pakistan to return to Afghanistan. Often these are family of the men actually involved in *jihad*. Occasionally men step out of the *jihad* for awhile, settle and support their families in Pakistan and wait to participate in the fighting again some years later. People do sometimes return to Afghanistan, not because they have become reconciled to the government or situation there, but rather because they find they do not like Pakistan and have nowhere else to go.

The *mujahidin* group composed of the Ferghanachi has operated in northern Afghanistan since 1982. The men most involved in forming the *mujahid* group did not believe that the Ferghanachis should simply go to Saudi Arabia because Afghanistan was not their real homeland. They saw the struggle in Afghanistan not only as against continuation of Soviet imperialism first witnessed by their parents but also as the opportunity for the creation of a transformed society in Afghanistan.

The Ferghanachi *mujahidin* group is also known as the *grup-i malaika*, the angel group, for their devotion to God. It is reported that the people in the countryside admire them for their Islamic observance. They are popular, it is said, because they always pay for the food and supplies they need. The group has been supplied by the political party of Gulbuddin Hekmatyar *Hizb-i Islami,* one of the Peshawar-based Islamic Revolutionary parties with especially close ties to Saudi Arabia. This party is known to have its basis of support in detribalized Pashtuns as Hekmatyar is of this background. Because of their anti-Pashtun sentiments, it seems unusual for the Ferghanachi group to be affiliated with Hizb. However, there are several reasons which make this more logical than it might first appear.

Hizb has always been well funded by Saudi Arabian sources and the large Ferghanachi community in Saudi Arabia has also provided funds for the *mujahid* group and for those temporarily in Pakistan. Perhaps a Saudi connection is important for the group to maintain. For some years, a Ferghanachi in the Hizb inner circle was instrumental in insuring that the group always received arms, an important consideration in the early 1980s. Some Ferghanachis were personally acquainted with Hekmatyar either because he is from Kunduz province originally or from his time at Kabul University. Personal knowledge of a person is important in maintaining trust and loyalty. Ferghanachi men of the first Afghan-born generation are generally committed to an Islamic revolutionary government in Afghanistan because they see the possibilities for social justice and progress in Islam. They do not favor a return to the *status quo ante* April 1978 because they perceive the Musahiban dynasty as essentially corrupt and also discriminatory against non-Pashtuns.

Since Hizb operates in northern Afghanistan, Hekmatyar has formulated a policy of advocating the liberation of the Muslim areas in Central Asia. Some fighting allegedly occurred on the northern side of the Amu Darya and Soviet

Muslims were reported to be joining the Afghan resistance in some cases. Hekmatyar's policy appeals to those who view the area north of the Amu Darya as their homeland who have always hoped that the Communist regime there would be overthrown. Hizb maps on display at the Afghanistan Studies Center at the University of Nebraska, Omaha, label the former Soviet Central Asian republics as Muslim-occupied territories, which coincides with an ideological commitment to return those areas to a legitimate Islamic government.[1] Burhanuddin Rabbani's party *Jamiat-i Islami* has many of the same policies regarding the former Soviet republics in Central Asia and the need for an Islamic government in Afghanistan. This party is supported by many Ferghanachis, particularly those who do not trust Pashtuns under any circumstances. However supplies for the *mujahid* group were always funneled through Hizb. Some Ferghanachis active in the resistance may have joined other *mujahid* groups affiliated with Jamiat but less data is available on these individuals. Informants indicated that of the Ferghanachi *mujahids* who lived in *mahalla* Kasani, half have been martyred.

### Life in Karachi

Informants estimated that perhaps only 150 Ferghanachi families were currently in Karachi. Most Ferghanachis have settled in several of the low socio-economic urban neighborhoods in Karachi. The areas are known by Pakistanis as Afghan areas and centers for the drug trade. Occasionally the Pakistani newspapers carry brief press reports on drug arrests from these areas and they are sometimes used as locations for Pakistani television shows when this kind of environment is needed in a drama. Some years ago, one of the Afghan areas known as a center for the heroin trade was bulldozed by the Pakistani police. Innocent and guilty all lost their homes. All that remains is the garbage and the ruins of two mosques. Many of the people, however, returned to the area after a while and rebuilt in adjoining neighborhoods.

These neighborhoods are mixed ethnically and include Pakistanis, Pathans, Afghan Pashtuns and various Tajik and Uzbek speaking groups from Afghanistan. In particular, in addition to the Ferghanachis from Kunduz, Baghlan, Khanabad and Kabul, there are Afghan Uzbeks from Mazar-i Sharif, Aqcha and Imam Sahib.

There is little close interaction between Pakistanis and the Ferghanachis. While men and boys have some interethnic business dealings through the marketplace, women generally do not have contact with outsiders. Pakistani girls who have become acquainted with Ferghanachi girls through school occasionally attend the latter's social gatherings or go shopping with them. Ferghanachi women invite Afghan Pashtun and Afghan Uzbek and Tajik women to their celebrations if they are known as good neighbors. These women sometimes drop in for visits but otherwise there is no prolonged interaction. For the most part, the circle of kinship and friendship is closed around the Ferghanachis though there is intermarriage, especially with Afghan Uzbeks.[2]

The areas in which Afghans live in Karachi are typically divided into several adjoining neighborhoods which include a square business area with rows of high rise flats above and the small stores, stalls and transportation center on the ground level. Within the same area other neighborhoods have more village-like dwellings with mud brick walls and household compounds which have grown up as squatter settlements, though with payment to Pakistani landowners. Areas with men living in tents are also located in the squatter settlements.

While the village household compounds rely on wells and residents may bring in electricity from the city on their own, the high-rise flats are of basic concrete construction with piped water, electricity, ceiling fans and gas. There are two flats on each side of a landing. The women therefore consider it ideal if members of the same ethnic group live in the four flats on the same level because women's celebrations may then spill over into all the flats without any concerns about modesty and veiling. However, often the situation is that a family is not surrounded by co-ethnics and therefore veiling behavior is necessary upon leaving the flat. Frequently, the women will leave the face open as they descend to the ground level and only as they exit the stairs and approach the ground level with all the shops full of men and boys will they cover their faces completely.

Each flat is identical to the others and contains two small sitting/sleeping rooms, a kitchen, a washroom, a bathroom and an entryway. The flat in which I stayed was home to ten adults over the age of 15 including one invalid old man. The sitting rooms contain windows on one wall and one of these rooms opens onto a small balcony which the women usually enclose with a curtain. They are then able to use the area for storage without veiling since no one can then see into the area. Because the windows of each flat are located only on one side, depending on its floor and the direction it faces, poor general lighting and lack of sunlight are common problems.

The people frequently arrive with few belongings. Over time they accumulate bedding, cooking utensils, plates, tea cups and clothing much as they had in Afghanistan. A nice carpet covering the floor, neatly painted walls, florescent lights, and modern sinks attached to pipes are signs that years have been spent in the same flat. There were people who had resided in the same flat for nine years.

The household compounds in the squatter settlements are similar in architecture and structure to typical rural and urban compounds in Afghanistan except that sometimes they have tin roofs and generally the amount of land is less. The great advantage to living in these is that there is land for a garden and for a few animals, either cows or sheep and perhaps chickens. The women in these compounds have more access to sunlight and the outdoors than do the women in the flats. However, the women in the flats say that insects are worse in the household compounds. Since garbage is thrown out of windows of the flats and sewage runs down to the ground floor where it accumulates and adjacent land is used as a city dump, insects are a significant problem in all areas. Mosquitos and flies are especially bothersome. Mosquito netting is sometimes used in the household compounds around sleeping areas. Diseases from various insect carriers including malaria are endemic. These poor material conditions in which people live are often compared to their previous situation in Afghanistan. The unsanitary streets, the insects, the heat, and the difficulties with keeping the households clean are all attributed to living in Pakistan not in Afghanistan where it was not like this, they said. Often they would say, "This is the way it is when one is a *musafir.*"

The women and girls complain about the physical conditions of their lives in ways that emphasize sadness and depression. For example, nearly every day, someone would say in Dari, "*diq shodam,*" I have become sad. Usually the sadness is attributed to environmental constraints: no place to go outside, too much darkness, small rooms, too much noise and confusion coming from the bazaar below. Women also speak of being unwell for long periods of time which again they attribute to their living situation in Pakistan. Minor illnesses such as headaches, colds, prolonged coughing (probably bronchitis), and diarrhea are common. One 21-year-old girl has developed severe leg pains which have been diagnosed by a Pakistani doctor as sciatica. Again these health problems are generally explained as the consequence of being *musafir.*

Most of the Ferghanachi men own and operate stores in the bazaar areas near their homes, a continuation of their urban merchant class occupational status. Women who had worked out of their homes in Afghanistan continued to earn their own meager income. One widow in her forties had sewed clothes for women clients in Kunduz even before her husband died. In Pakistan she specializes in fancy dresses, bridal gowns, celebration dresses using dress catalogs from abroad for ideas just as she had in Afghanistan. This woman has purchased a new foot pedal sewing machine for 2000 rupees ($100) and obtains commissions from customers several times a week. The clients provide their own material. However, two or three days of work on a dress results in only 50 rupees payment ($2-3) because many women can do this work and therefore will not pay much for the service, she says. Women also sell embroidery. There is also a woman mullah who writes Quranic verses for use in curing. Generally, there are few opportunities other than these for women to earn their own income.

The people believe that one reason they have come to Karachi is that housing and living expenses in the urban areas of Peshawar and Islamabad are more expensive. Unlike the refugee camps in which people are given food rations as part

of humanitarian aid, these unregistered people are self-sufficient in fulfilling their
dietary needs. Often people buy food items like eggs and cream nearly every day in
the bazaar. Women in the tenement flats have no ovens and cannot bake bread, so
this is another item that is purchased daily. Both the long flat Pashtun bread and
the round Uzbek sourdough bread are available from bakers in the local
neighborhoods. In the household compounds, traditional ovens, *tandurs,* are constructed. Women then can bake bread for their own use and for celebrations.

The varieties of Uzbek foods still prepared for social gatherings are a source of
prestige and pride. Uzbeks in Karachi, like their counterparts in Central Asia,
Afghanistan and abroad, still make many noodle dishes such as *mantu,* a steamed
meat-filled dumpling which requires a special cooker. Women in Karachi make the
following kinds of food items which may be traced back to Central Asian origins:
bread with fat cracklings; onion bread; *kolcha,* small rounds of bread; *patir,* bread
with milk and oil; *samsa,* fried dumplings; *qatlama,* layered fried dough; *lagman,* a
noodle dish; *pilaw,* rice with meat, onions and carrots; various soups and
vegetables. Black tea is generally used but, as some prefer green tea, it is also
widely available both for everyday use and celebrations. As in Afghanistan,
occasionally the traditional water pitcher was brought around so that guests could
rinse their hands before and after eating. The retention of ethnic foods and rituals
surrounding food is a major cultural symbol for the Ferghanachis wherever their
location.

## Women's Rituals

Within the traditional urban neighborhoods in Afghanistan, women's relationships of kinship and friendship connected households together and provided daily
interaction and intimacy. Because of the close physical proximity of the flats in the
Karachi areas where the Ferghanachis live and even the relatively nearby location
of those in the household compounds, this aspect of women's lives has been
retained. Despite strict veiling patterns, women visit each other frequently during
the day and at night. They are careful when walking to keep to the areas near the
stairs rather than to the open areas. When they visit those in the household
compounds, they usually arrange taxi or rickshaw transportation. Women while
veiled will go shopping in the bazaar to purchase cloth or other items. Unmarried
girls have their own subcommunity with gatherings, sleepovers, and special
friendships, again the same pattern as in Afghanistan. Teenage girls are permitted
while veiled to occasionally take the public buses, which have special women's
sections in the front, and go to shop in other parts of town.

Ferghanachi women use the Afghan veil, the full covering with built-in mesh
over the eyes, called *chadari* in Afghanistan or *burqa* in Pakistan. Equally common

in Karachi are the various types of *hijab*, the modest dress used in Saudi Arabia which often includes a black ankle-length cloak which buttons in the front and a separate black face veil. The use of the *hijab* is of practical and symbolic significance. Women point out that the *hijab* is of lighter weight than the *chadari* and that it is much more comfortable to wear in Karachi's heat. Many women have visited Saudi Arabia and are in Pakistan only to return to Saudi Arabia again with legal permission.[3] These women already have purchased and are comfortable wearing the *hijab* and do not want to wear the *chadari*. Women whose political sympathies are with either Jamiat-i Islami or Hizb-i Islami, the Islamic Revolutionary parties, may also be wearing these veils to suggest either Islamic solidarity or their support of the cause of the Islamic Revolution. Although the Ferghanachi women did not say that this was a reason for the wearing of the *hijab*, the fact that the Ferghanachi *mujahid* group is affiliated with Hizb-i Islami may be a factor in this practice.

Just as in Afghanistan, the women's community is organized around life crisis celebrations. Since these celebrations always include a meal, close friends and neighbors of the hostesses always help in food preparation. The life crisis rituals of most importance in Karachi are those surrounding marriage, obviously critical in assuring continuity and stability of families in a time of great social change and upheaval. It seems as if much care is taken to find a bride for a young man either before he moves permanently to Saudi Arabia or before he returns to fight in Afghanistan.

The rituals surrounding marriage traditionally begin with the engagement period, a phase which is often truncated in Karachi. In Afghanistan, the betrothal period frequently lasted for months and prolonged negotiations occurred about the timing of the wedding and the various gifts and brideprice from the groom's side to the bride. There are cases in Pakistan in which the betrothal period is less than a week and mothers are frantic about arranging the appropriate food and clothes for their daughters' wedding celebrations. As in Afghanistan, the engagement is marked by the ritual presentation of bridegifts in which clothing, material, toiletries, jewelry, and linens are given to the bride by the women on the groom's side. The gifts are brought in trunks and suitcases and a respected woman opens each gift and shows it to the audience with explanations of the giver and where it was obtained.

Traditionally, three successive celebrations were part of marriage itself: the celebration of the night of the henna when the bride's hands are decorated with henna and she is adorned with cosmetics by the groom's female relatives in preparation for meeting him; the celebration of the night of the *nikah* or contract, when the groom escorts the bride to his home; and the *yuz achti* the next afternoon when the bride greets the community of women of whom she is the newest member. All three of these are basically intact in Karachi although in one case the groom has refused to have the henna celebration. Whether this is because he is "modern" or because he is "cheap" was privately discussed among the women. In Pakistan the henna is sometimes done in a special non-traditional way. There is a women's bazaar which is in a building closed to men. In the women's bazaar are Pakistani hair stylists, women who specialize in drawing the popular henna designs, cosmetic experts, and women's accessory, underwear and clothing sales. The bride's friends may escort her to have her hair, makeup and henna done by these experts rather than doing these activities in the traditional way.

In Karachi there is a stricter enforcement of traditional norms by the local Ferghanachi religious leaders. No live entertaiment at women's celebrations is permitted although such entertainment was permitted in Afghanistan *(See Chapter 6)*. The women therefore use the *daira,* the tambourine-like drum, (*chirmanda-*Uzbek) and cassette tapes for music to accompany their dancing. The effect of this is to decrease the level of participation in the dancing in some cases. In the Ferghanachi communities of Saudi Arabia and the United States, rented halls or hotels are used for the wedding celebrations. According to the women, in Karachi

*Photo 8.1*
*The*
*Ethnographer*
*in*
*Karachi,*
*Pakistan*

this also is not permitted by the religious authorities because of the presence of many men with bad reputations in the local hotels. In all locations, the single most important wedding symbol that has been retained is the Uzbek wedding song *"Yar Yar."* In Pakistan, as in Afghanistan, this song is performed by the women as the bride is escorted from inside her mother's household.

Another change in Karachi is the early celebration of the *kilenchaqirdi* (bride-welcoming), perhaps the most common type of gathering in the Karachi Ferghanachi women's community. In Afghanistan a longer transitional period of perhaps 40 days was followed when women visited the bride in her new home, the bride not going outside nor attending *kilenchaqirdis* immediately after the marriage rituals. However, in Karachi *kilenchaqirdis* are held within the next few days after the *nikah* perhaps because in some cases the brides or the women wanting to honor her would be leaving soon. As a special guest, a bride receives presents from her hostesses at the end of the *kilenchaqirdi.*

One problem the women have in continuing these celebrations is that small details and niceties of the customs seem frequently to be lost even though the overall events and themes remain. All rites of passage celebrations traditionally began with *chichilla*, the strewing of candy or coins over the person whose status change is marked as she enters the room where the celebration is held. A bride thus entering the *yuz achti* or the *kilenchaqirdi* would have *chichilla;* other women and children guests would scramble for the lucky candy, and then the bride, after having been escorted to the place of honor, would *salaam*, bow, to those assembled. If any other guests arrived later, the bride would rise and *salaam* to them also. *Chichilla* and the *salaam* to the guests are frequently not done in Karachi sometimes because people say they forgot and sometimes because people say they do not want to bother to make the bride behave properly.

Also changed in Karachi was the distribution of mementos at the end of women's celebrations. In Afghanistan, women guests were always given a memento or remembrance of the occasion by the hostesses. These consisted of scarves, or more typically, small embroidered handkerchiefs publically presented at the end of the celebration. Women might give out scores of these at a celebration at their house and would have scores of them that they had received at various celebrations. While this does occur in Karachi, some women are unable to participate because as new arrivals, they simply do not have the handkerchiefs to give away nor can they afford to purchase such items. Those who have been settled in Karachi longer or are wealthier are able to make these distributions.

Generally, women's gatherings held inside are of necessity smaller than comparable gatherings in Afghanistan. The sitting rooms of the flats are smaller than the household compounds of Afghanistan and no more than 30-50 women fit in the two sitting rooms of each flat. Sometimes the overflow is seated in the interior entry or in a neighbor's flat if it belongs to a co-ethnic. Because the henna and *nikah* celebrations typically include over 100 guests and range to perhaps 300, they have to be held in the areas where the traditional household compounds are found, not in the flats. The other type of gathering which is common are those in which a women mullah does readings from the Quran. Though this type of gathering was held in Afghanistan, it seems more frequent in Karachi perhaps because of the heightened religiosity of the *jihad/hijrat* situation.

## NOTES

1. Eden Naby comments (1984:13-16, 1986a:147) that the concern for the liberation of Soviet Muslims dates back to at least 1929 during the reign of Habibullah II. For information on the Afghan resistance's influence on Soviet Muslims, see Bennigsen 1984.

2. Intermarriage with Saudis takes place in Saudi Arabia, another indication that resettlement there is likely to be permanent.

3. With the strong Ferghanachi community already in Saudi Arabia, women, especially those with small children, use haj passports to leave Afghanistan rather than making the arduous journey to Pakistan. The women do not intend to return to Afghanistan at the end of the haj period and remain under the protection of their relatives in Saudi Arabia. However, they cannot stay in that country legally. They then go to Pakistan to make arrangements to return to Saudi Arabia officially.

# Chapter 9

## Exhortation to *Jihad*

The daily life of the people in Karachi is even more imbued with the ambience of Islamic observance than it had been in Afghanistan. Though the Ferghanachis were known for their piety in Afghanistan having been *muhajir* once before, in Karachi there is more time devoted to prayer and religious study by many including women. Both Hizb-i Islami and Jamiat-i Islami run schools in the neighborhoods which include religious training. Boys attend these in the mornings. Girls frequently do not attend school. Often teenage boys have additional religious instruction from the local religious scholars and Ferghanachi mosque leaders as well.

In addition to the five daily prayers, some people devote much time to the recitation of *duaa,* special prayers for a specific purpose, such as the freedom or the establishment of an Islamic state in Afghanistan. People also read and study the Quran for hours at a time and make much use of Persian language books about Islam and proper behavior. In one family there was a discussion of the works of the Persian writer Saadi and the teenage boys, in particular, discussed the rhymed couplets of his stories and put them in an Islamic context.

Another source of Islamic discussion for many are the numerous cassettes[1] that circulate which offer education about the importance of the *jihad.* These *tabligh-i jihad* cassette tapes, mostly in Dari, may be played for hours and include numerous stories based on the Quran and hadith which explain the sacrifices people must be prepared to make during the time of *jihad.* The cassettes,[1] made in Afghanistan, usually are taped while one of the local religious scholars and teachers is preaching a public sermon about the *jihad.* The tapes are then brought into Pakistan and sold or exchanged at the same stores where music casettes are available. Sometimes these cassettes have folk music and rhymes against the current Afghan regime. Even when the cassettes are played many times, the effective ones elicit further discussion on Islamic observance, beliefs and *jihad.* Among the discussions that resulted from listening to these tapes was one about the validity of prayer. Someone asked whether a prayer would be invalidated if one were praying to God so intently that one did not realize blood was flowing from an unrecognized injury. There is much concern with the form and the intent of prayer. Discussion of the placement of the feet, proper washing, and sincerity are common topics.

*Mujahidin* publications are widely read. People are familiar with the political parties based in Peshawar and there is some discussion regarding their inability to

*Photo 9.1  The Sayid Harun Shahid <u>mujahid</u> group from the martyrdom booklet c. 1990.*

*Photo 9.2  Page from the martyrdom booklet c. 1990.*

cooperate. Loyalty of the people toward a specific *mujahidin* group seems to be based primarily on local regional and ethnic ties. The Ferghanachis in Karachi thus are intensely loyal to and involved with their own *mujahid* group named after Sayid Harun Shahid. People have relatives and neighbors in the group, and they have pictures of participants and martyrs on the walls and in memory books. People secondarily speak with admiration for certain field commanders in Afghanistan such as the famous Massoud who was very successful against the Russians and the Afghan government in the Panjshir and in the north.

Many of the boys hold cards from the political party Jamiat-i Islami (Rabbani's party) but there seems little personal attachment to it. In fact, since the Sayid Harun Shahid group is supplied by Hizb-i Islami (Hetmatyar's group), one might have expected them to have Hizb cards but none do. Their explanation is that it was much easier and quicker to obtain Jamiat cards in Peshawar. Though they seem not that emotionally attached to either Jamiat or Hizb, they are unquestionably committed to the *jihad* and to the idea of becoming martyrs for Islam. "Afghanistan azad shavad; Shahid shavam; haram mimuram, Let Afghanistan become free; Let me be a martyr; I will die properly," said one 15-year-old.

The people generally attempt to minimize disputes between the *mujahidin* parties. They often refuse to pick between Hizb and Jamiat saying that when the time came and a good government has come to Afghanistan all this will be resolved. However, there is discussion of the fact that when two boys got into a fight in the street, their fathers came not to break up the fight but to fight themselves because one was in Hizb and one in Jamiat. One 17-year-old boy often jokingly referred to as a future mullah deprecated the fact that one no longer spoke of people as good Muslims, the only important criterion, but with which political party they are affiliated.

The three most crucial Islamic concepts that occupy the minds of the people and were discussed nearly daily were *jihad, shahid*, and *qiyamat*. These inter-related concepts resonate with popular knowledge of the Islamic worldview and history. *Jihad* refers not only to active warfare but to any struggle for the sake of Islam including working for a good and just society in peacetime (Canfield 1989:23). It also refers to the inner struggle whereby one works on becoming a good person. *Shahid* is generally translated as martyr for the sake of Islam, but it is contains the concept of witness as in the *shahada*, the recitation of the creed that there is but one God and Muhammad is the prophet of God. One who is witness to the faith and submits even unto death is thus *shahid*. The *qiyamat* is the time of the last judgment when all humans will be called forth from their graves and will be judged by God. One who is *shahid* goes to paradise and is thus spared the agonies of hell at the time of the judgment.

There are many stories of martyrs which circulate among people. These are inspirational and frequently repeated to illustrate admirable qualities. Often a person who will be *shahid* knows it in advance and can prepare for death.

> One night a man had a dream that his head was carried in his hands as he approached God at the *qiyamat*. So he went to the *mawlewi* to ask what the dream meant and he was told that he would be *shahid* the next day and to prepare by putting on good clothes and purifying himself carefully. He did this and the next day his head was blown off. So the story came from his companions there to his family and relatives in Pakistan (an informant).

The unstated part of the story understood by everyone is that at the time of the *qiyamat*, the man's head will be returned and thus he will carry it before God and it will provide a visible symbol of his martyrdom. God will even pardon the sins of relatives for the sake of the *shahid*. Visible symbols are important in the recognition of the *shahid*. Therefore the *shahid* is buried in his bloody battle clothes, not in a shroud. It is believed that no pain is felt in the deathblow and that the corpse of the *shahid* does not rot. It is considered an honorable, proper and beautiful death. The pictures of 27 *shahids* were in the martyrdom booklet that was circulating in Karachi in 1990. Twenty-one were from Kunduz and four were from Baghlan. Most of the dead were between the ages of 15 and 25. Their deaths occurred between 1982 and 1988 with most of them at the battle for Kunduz when the *mujahids* captured the city after the Soviet withdrawal.

The following text is a excerpted translation of one of the popular cassette tapes on *jihad* that was circulating in Karachi in 1989-90. It is presented in several portions with commentary and interpretation after each section.

# I

**. . . Brothers of Islam! It is obvious you know what a martyr is. There is no ablution for a martyr. The person martyred in the path of God does not need a shroud. They are buried in their bloody clothing; they go into the grave in clothes full of blood. They are the ones who will come out of their graves on the day of judgment to the plains of judgment while their blood flows. Even then their blood will be fresh. Only the appearance is blood but the fragrance of musk and ambergris comes from the blood. The fragrance of the martyrs' blood will envelop the entire plain of judgment . . .**

**A martyr is a person who will not give up his soul unless he sees his place in the heavens. After a martyr is wounded and his body is laid upon the ground, houris come down from heaven and sit by his head. A houri puts his**

head in her lap . . . and with a silky material she wipes the dust from his face and she says, "Oh martyr of the path of God, look at me. I was waiting for you. I was waiting for you." The martyr sees his face reflected in the houri's face. He asks, "Who are you that I see my own face in your face?" Then she says, "I am the houri who was waiting for you. I was asking the merciful God when will this brave Muslim join me. It was God's decision that now you have joined me. Now there is no sorrow or sadness in front of you." At that moment as he looks up, the crystal lights of heaven call him and the doors of the highest part of heaven call him and all the doors of heaven are open to him. Houris show gifts of forgiveness from God. Angels are standing in rows in front of him, saying, "welcome, welcome. Come! Everything is waiting for you. The heavens are waiting for you. The houris are waiting for you. The angels are in rows waiting for you."

. . . The Prophet (Peace Be Upon Him) says, "On the Day of Judgment, God will give a crown for martyrs, for martyrs' parents and for martyrs' relatives." At the day of judgment, a martyr can intercede for seventy people. The martyr can take seventy relatives who were in hell to heaven. It is fortunate for Muslims. God asked the martyrs of Badr and Uhud,[2] "Oh martyrs of the path of Islam, you people who give your soul, your blood, your wealth, your children, and your wives in my path; Oh people to whom eternal life is already given, where God's blessing is already given to you; Oh people, who fought to make Me happy and have done so, what do you want from Me? What is your wish? Tell Me if you have any desires and I will grant them for you." They reply, "You have given us all blessings. That you are pleased with us is everything to us. We do not have any other wishes. We have achieved our desires; we have reached our aspirations; we have attained the pinnacle of our lives;[3] at this time, we have no other wishes. God asks again, "Request something." Then they understand that God will not leave them alone [until they respond] so they ask God, "The only thing we want is for You to take us back to the world in order to fight against the unbelievers until we die again in Your path. Give us this blessing again." What is God's reply to this? He says, "My special and unique servants, be content. It is not your God's habit to return you to the world, full of sorrow and sadness; that world full of sin, that world where you spent days and nights full of worries. Days and nights you were trying to cleanse your sins; days and nights you tried to order the chaos but could not succeed. I will never take you back to that world full of all those sins and impurity. It is not your God's custom. Now you have entered My blessing." Then the martyrs call again and say, "We know you will not take us there but we wish there was somebody to take the news of our condition back to the world to our fellow Muslim brothers. We wish to tell them not to die under the blanket. They should be informed to fight against the unbelievers until martyrdom. Come to us! We will be satisfied at the time when you become martyrs and join us. Become martyrs and let your blood flow and your face and feet be full of dust from the *jihad*, and the houris of heaven will wipe off that dust with a silken cloth" . . .

In this section, the speaker explains martyrdom using imagery familiar to his audience. The martyr who dies for God's sake without thought of personal reward does in fact achieve a reward at the time of the last judgment. He achieves paradise for his relatives as well as himself. Not only does his bloody wound protect him from the decay of natural death, his blood smells of perfume. Houris care for him and he sees the wonder of heaven. The martyr's request is that he be allowed to die for God once again, but this cannot be. Through the words of the speaker, martyrs speak to their relatives and friends left behind, urging them to likewise give their lives. The speaker quotes both God and the Prophet Muhammad to reinforce his points. What seems to be a terrible and sad end, death, becomes an occasion for rejoicing when the death is one of martyrdom.

## II

Now I will tell you a story from the beginning of Islam about a woman. I tell you a story about the bravery of a woman. On the day of the battle of Uhud, Nasia bint Kahf Yazdi, (one of the Muslim scholars Shah Abdul Haq Dehlavi gave the name as Nasiba, but in most books, it is Nasia), who was an old woman, was among the fighters. She was carrying a leather water pouch on her back. She had a bowl for water in her hand and she was distributing water in that battle with her own hand. It was a time when the fierce battle had started. See what Nasia says. She had a son who was a participant in the battle. She herself was distributing water to the *ghazis*. This was the highest honor given to this old woman. This is a woman who the Prophet mentioned in his hadiths, that is, the Prophet has mentioned her in his words. May God give this kind of courage to all women in Afghanistan. Nasia Bint Kahf Yazdi was distributing water to the *ghazis* when she saw the battle was very fierce. She stopped distributing water. She actually participated in the battle. She stood in front of the Prophet as a shield to protect him [even though] she had a bent back. While she was involved in the battle, one of her sons was wounded and came to her. He fell down in front of her. The Prophet called upon her and said, "Mother! Nasia!" She replied, "[I am your] sacrifice. May my father and mother be your sacrifice. Oh master, what is your command?" The Prophet [said], "Brave woman of Islam, brave Muslim woman, you are so courageous. You are so brave. You are a woman where not too many men would have your bravery. Oh, Nasia! Put some ointment on your son's wounds." Nasia took her scarf, tore a piece of it, bound up the wound of her son and said, "My dear son, I see your pulse is still beating. It is not necessary for you to lie down in front of your mother. I do not need a cowardly son. Fight the unbelievers until the time you have given your life for Islam. Until that time you have not sacrificed yourself for Islam. I do not need a son like you, a coward who comes and lies down in front of me. It is only one wound you have. Get up, my dear son." She took one of his arms, raised him up and led him onto the battlefield. She fought in the Uhud mountains until her son was martyred. After he was martyred, the Prophet called and said, "Oh Nasia! Your son is martyred, but I will point out his killer." When Nasia looked [she saw] her son's killer was a very fierce unbeliever. In that moment, they said, "This is the man who killed your son. Do not let him go." Nasia took her sword, raised it, and hit the head of the man, shouting, "God is great." The man was split into two pieces. When the unbeliever lay dead on the ground, the Prophet said, "Oh Nasia! What a brave woman you are!" When Nasia (had) raised her sword and hit the man, she saw the Prophet smiling. Then she asked the Prophet, "Why are you smiling?" He replied, "Your wielding the sword was so wonderful, you have left no dark spot in the Islamic struggle. The way you threw the sword was so wonderful that it will remain on your name. Everybody will mention it until the day of judgment. Oh brave woman of Islam, be confident that you received the mercy of God and the Prophet." Listen to Nasia's reply. She says, "When I saw the Prophet smiling," (she took the end of his shirttail), she says, "it seems as though you like the way a bent old woman fights and are happy about it." He said, "Yes. I know you are a very brave woman." He asked, "Why are you holding my shirttail?" [She said,] "I have one wish." He said, "What's your wish?" She said, "Pray for me that on the day of judgment I am your neighbor, that I am with you, your family and all your descendants." He replied, "God has accepted your wish." This was a woman who sacrificed in the way of Islam. She lived for awhile longer and then she died the time of Abu Bakr.

Nasia represents the best kind of behavior of those in a desperate battle for right against overwhelming odds. She exemplifies self-sacrifice. The speaker has chosen the story of this woman because it is quite remarkable, given women's traditional involvement with household and kinship, that a woman would urge her son, probably her dearest relative, to become a martyr. Nasia has transcended narrow family concerns and even actively fights and kills an unbeliever for the good of the community. Her behavior is praised by the Prophet and rewarded by God. Toward the beginning of the section, the speaker made a short prayer, "May God give this kind of courage to all women in Afghanistan." By this, the speaker means the women of Afghanistan must be willing to make the kind of sacrifice Nasia made. Islam and community must mean more to them than their own families.

### III

I will tell you a story of a young man named Hanzala. He was a young man for whom the Prophet had contracted a young girl [in marriage]. The Prophet called his name. He said. "[May I be your] sacrifice. Let Hanzala be your sacrifice and let Hanzala's bride of one night be your sacrifice." He asked the Prophet if he is permitted to spend the night with his new bride as the next day they are preparing to go to the battle of Uhud. Hanzala's bride was given to him. The young man held his bride's hand and went to his house. He spent the night with the bride. The next day he was taking a bath to purify himself. He put the container of water next to himself, put one bowlful of water on his head and at that moment, he heard the voice of an angel saying, "The Prophet spent his night in the middle of the mountains and sands of Uhud and you are enjoying your night with your bride. Oh Hanzala! Has your conscience accepted this? Oh Hanzala! Do you think you have enough time to purify yourself?" Hanzala decides, "I can not wait. I cannot purify myself. I must go to Uhud in a state of impurity." As he started going to Uhud while he was impure, his bride of one night came out, grabbed his hand and asked, "Oh Hanzala! Last night I dreamed that they were taking you to the skies. I know that you will be martyred but since you spent the night with me, are there any people around to witness this [the fact that he was impure]?" They found four women. In front of these four she said, "Oh Muslim women. Be witness to this. I got you as witnesses to tell the Prophet that this one night king of mine has spent the night with me. He has slept next to me for a night and the next day he was not able to do the purification. In his enthusiasm, he is going to Uhud. I have dreamed that this one night king of mine was taken to the skies. From the dream I know he will be martyred." She grabbed Hanzala's hands, and holding them, said, "Today there are hundreds of brides left with their hands in henna and thousands of grooms with hennaed hands are martyred. Thousands and thousands of brides are left behind. The young are martyred." Oh citizens of Afghanistan, Oh citizens who are lying down in blood and dirt, what is left for you and me? Still we are not seeking ways to maintain the religion. Still we do not repent.

So Hanzala, the one night groom, was going to Uhud. His bride grabbed his hand and said. "Oh my one night king, are you leaving me alone? Are you going from me? Will we see each other on the day of judgment. According to my dream, this is the last time [I will see] you go." Hanzala faced his bride and said, "Oh my one night bride, pardon me, I am in love with the Prophet. I am the servant of the messenger of God. I am the special slave of God. Is it fair if I sleep next to you while the Prophet is in the mountains and sands of Uhud with the other *mujahidin* involved in *jihad*? Should Hanzala lie by his bride enjoying the moment? Pardon me for this. We will see each other on the day of judgment. On the day of judgment, ask God and the Prophet for me [since they will be able to find me]. Oh my one night bride, I will not forget you. Maybe you will be able to find me on that day. You will find me on the plains of judgment. You may find me in bloody clothes. Oh my one night bride, you will smell the musk and fragrance from my blood." He said goodbye and went on toward Uhud. The bride stayed in Medina. She lay prostrate on the ground from the sorrow of her groom's [departure].

When he got to Uhud, this young man looked at the Prophet's eyes. The Prophet saw this young man Hanzala coming toward him. He said, "Oh Hanzala, did you leave your bride at home and come here?" He replied, "[I am your] sacrifice. Do you think Hanzala is a coward? Do you think Hanzala is without courage? Do you think Hanzala should sleep next to his bride while the Prophet and his followers fight in the mountains and sands of Uhud? Do you think Hanzala could bear this shame? Hanzala is your slave; he is not a coward. The love of martyrdom has brought me here. I left my one night bride to the shelter of the only God." At that moment, he drew his sword and entered the battleground. Then the news came to the Prophet that Hanzala was impure. He was martyred while impure. He fought until he was martyred. Then the companions came to the Prophet and said, "[We are your] sacrifice. You said there is no ablution for martyrs, but there is cleansing for the impure. As Hanzala's wife got four women as witnesses that he did not purify himself--he was too impatient to purify himself--he came to Uhud without purifying so we should wash him now." The Prophet said, "You do not know the extent [to which] a martyr [becomes pure]. The angels came from heaven and already are washing his body." When they went to see Hanzala, they saw water flowing from his head to his feet. The angels washed and cleansed him. The Prophet buried him in the sands of Uhud.

On the tape, as the speaker recounts the poignant scene between Hanzala and his bride, some weeping and sobbing can be discerned. The speaker's goal in telling this story is to reinforce his earlier point about martyrdom. Even the men who come to the Prophet Muhammad with the news of Hanzala's death are not aware of the purity of the martyr. They believe that because Hanzala died without purifying himself after sexual intercourse he should be washed. But the Prophet points out that the angels are already performing that task. The other point of this story carries over the preceding one about Nasia. Brides must be willing to lose their husbands just as mothers must be willing to lose sons.

## IV

Again [I tell] another story from the battle of Uhud. I will tell you a story of two *mujahids* on the day of the Uhud battle. One was Sa'ad ibn Abi Waqqas and the other was Abdullah Ajash. They were both together praying in a remote section of Uhud when they agreed that one would pray and the other would say amen [ask for God to accept the prayer] and then vice versa. Abi Waqqas began first and Abdullah was saying amen. Abi Waqqas was saying, I want to fight against the unbelievers and I request to be counted as a *ghazi* and Abdullah said amen. When Abdullah's turn came, listen to what he says (he is the nephew of Amir Hamza). "Oh God, I want to fight against strong unbelievers. Give me the highest degree of martyrdom. After I become a martyr, I wish for the unbelievers to cut off my nose and ears, string them, display them to other unbelievers and say this is the nose and ears of Abdullah. On the harsh day of judgment when You bring me up, I do not want to have ears and nose. When You ask me what happened to your nose and ears, I shall reply, 'Oh God, I gave my nose and ears in the way of Your path.'" Both prayers were accepted by God. Both started fighting against the unbelievers. Sa'ad ibn Abi Waqqas was not martyred. He fought and finally he was numbered alive among the *ghazis*. In Abdullah's turn, he fought and fought and finally joined the martyrs. An unbeliever came and cut his nose and ears, strung them and showed them to his friends. That was the granting of both prayers. Sa'ad ibn Abi Waqqas said later, "I wish I had prayed the way Abdullah did. What a prayer and what an acceptance that we saw with our own eyes."

Now among the participants in Uhud were Hazrat Ali and Amir Hamza who was martyred. When Hamza was martyred, a woman from the other side named Hind, Abu Sufyan's wife, came and removed Hamza's liver. Actually he was killed by Hurya-i Wahshi. After Hurya killed Hamza, he instantaneously cut open his stomach, removed his liver and brought it to Hind because she sought vengeance. Because [Hamza] had killed her relative, when she received the liver, she bit and chewed it. She is notorious in all the religious books as Hind, the liver-eater.[4] What she did was based on animosity, but from the blood she swallowed, God later gave her guidance. What she did was God's will. It was because of the pure blood of a martyr that on the day when [Mecca] was conquered, Hind, her husband, Abu Sufyan, and her entire family became Muslims. See how people sacrifice in the way of Islam!

These are two stories linked together by the theme of bodily desecration after death. In a natural death as from old age, the worse consequences include for the body not to be intact and thus not properly buriable. Here the glory and potency of martyrdom reverses the normal feelings of repugnance at bodily mutilation. Abdullah Ajash requests to be martyred and mutilated and his request is granted. Even more than this, Amir Hamza is mutilated after death for the sake of a woman's revenge, but his liver, the mutilated object, becomes the agency of her redemption. Again the theme of the powerful nature of martyrdom is apparent.

## V

On the day of the battle of Uhud, as we should know, the Prophet lost his teeth. His uncle was also martyred that day. We as Muslims should know that this great religion of Islam has come to us at the price of the blood and the teeth of the Prophet. This religion has not come to us without charge. This religion came to us at the price of the blood of the Prophet and others in the mountains and the sands. It came from harshness not from ease (literally, carpets and bedding.) The Prophet and his companions sat on the rocks and sands of the mountains. As a consequence, this religion is not without cost--they did sacrifice. We should know that this religion has come to us at the price of the blood of the Prophet. When the Prophet's teeth were broken, the angel Gabriel came to him and said to him, "Oh Prophet, your God sends you greetings. The angels send blessings to every hair on your head. God also told me to tell you, His beloved messenger, [to] give this message [to you]. 'Oh My beloved one, you kept your broken teeth. Give them to Us and We will give you anything you want in exchange. What is the price of your teeth? Tell Us.'" He replied, "The price of my teeth is granting me the right to intercede for the *umma*, [community]. I will not give my teeth. I will keep them with me. On the day of judgment I will take these teeth and show them to You and I will ask. Since my teeth were martyred in the battle of Uhud and it has value for You, I will intercede for my *umma*. For the exchange of my teeth, You pardon the sins of my *umma*."
. . .

After the end of the battle of Uhud, they returned to Medina. Before they arrived, the women heard that the Prophet was killed in the battle and all were mourning for him. All were mourning for him. Among the mourners were Fatima, the Prophet's daughter. "Oh father, my children's grandfather, you were ready to listen to my children's woes. Now to whom can I turn? Now you are martyred so Gabriel will not return to our house anymore. You left me and now I am an orphan." There was another woman whose husband and four sons were at the battle. The woman came to Fatima and asked where she was going. She replied she was going to Uhud. The woman said, "It is not necessary for you to go. I will go and bring word of your father." Fatima said, "You may be too concerned with the news of your own husband and children. You may forget my father." The woman said, "What are you saying? I am not one of those cowardly women to forget my master." She went [to Uhud] and walked past the body of her own son. Somebody said, "That is your son on the ground there." She passed by the body of her brother. Someone said, "That is your brother on the ground." She said, "I do not care." She passed her husband's body and approached the Prophet. She saw that the Prophet was alive. [She said,] "Sacrifice to the messenger of God. No sorrow can overtake me. I care not about my children, husband or brother. May my husband, children and all my life be sacrificed to the Prophet. Thank God that you are alive. We can solve any difficulty but not if you left us. Oh Prophet, I have to return to your daughter Fatima with the news that you are alive." Then she walked toward Medina. She arrived at Fatima's house, entered and Fatima was waiting. Fatima asked the news. The woman said, "Be happy that you are not left an orphan. He was alive when I got to Uhud. I passed many bodies but he was alive. I bring the good news that your father is alive." Now the Prophet and his companions started coming down from the mountains of Uhud. Hajis have seen these mountains. May God give us our country back with peace under the Islamic *sharia* and all Muslims can visit the Uhud mountains.

The Prophet himself is injured at the battle of Uhud. However, like Hamza's mutilated liver, Muhammad's teeth become the instrument of redemption not just of one misguided individual but for the entire *umma*, Muslim community, for whom the Prophet gains permission to intercede at the time of the *qiyamat*. The possibility of Muhammad's death, indicated through his injury, would constitute an unimaginable loss to the entire community since God's revelations would no longer come via the angel Gabriel. The theme first laid out in the story of Nasia, that ordinary people must be willing to face and transcend the loss of kin, then comes into play. The woman who seeks news of Muhammad's rumored death ignores her own dead son, brother, and husband and is filled with joy for the sake of the community upon her discovery that the Prophet lives.

## VI

. . . Now listen to this story of Hamza's small daughter, also named Fatima. Now the old women who could not go to the battleground heard the *mujahids* were coming from Uhud. They took whatever they had, dates, some milk and went to greet the people who came from Uhud. Hamza's little daughter thought her father would be among those returning. She found some milk in the house, took that and found a handful of dates. She ran to greet her father Hamza. She did not know her father was martyred at Uhud. He was buried without a shroud. When they put him in the grave, they had only a small cloth to cover him. When his face was covered, his feet were bare; when his feet were covered, his face was bare. Although a martyr needs no shroud, he was chopped in pieces so they wanted to cover his body. Finally, the Prophet decided to cover his face with the cloth and his feet with thornbushes. The daughter does not know and she was running toward the crowd, feeling happy in the expectation of seeing her father. She expected her father to pick her up in his arms and talk sweetly. When she reached the crowd, she saw Abu Bakr who was in the front of the line.

She shouted and asked, "Oh Siddiq Abu Bakr, where is my father? What did you do to my father?" With his eyes full of tears, he said, "My sweet daughter, the Prophet is coming after me." He did not mention what happened to her father.[5] Then Fatima, Hamza's small daughter, started running around and finally she saw the Prophet. When she saw the Prophet, she said, "Where is my father? What did you do with my father?" The Prophet came down from his camel. The Prophet's whole body shook at the sight of the small girl. He began to cry. He held her, put her head on his chest and said, "Fatima, my uncle's orphan. Know that I am your father." She said, "From what you say, there is the smell of blood. Tell me the story of my father's martyrdom." He said, "You are not able to hear the story." The moment that he told her that her father was martyred, the pitcher of milk fell from her hand and the dates scattered. She was screaming and crying. She said, "At least you should have taken the milk and dates from my hand. We did not have even these few dates and I asked someone else to give them to me. Now you are not here to receive them." As I told you at the beginning of my speech, at this moment he appeared alive in the sky and greeted the Prophet. The Prophet asked him, "Where were you? I know you were martyred." He replied, "My daughter Fatima has brought me milk and dates and I could not come to receive them. I should not have allowed the pitcher

of milk to fall but I could not prevent it. Now I come to welcome my
daughter. I have a request of my master. I am content with what God has
done." The Prophet replied, "Oh my uncle, you who have nourished the
religion and the Prophet, what is your request? Your daughter has marked
our hearts. What is your request?" He calls from the air. "Fatima is an
orphan now. She has no one. Do not let her be alone. Do not let her be
without caresses." After hearing that, the Prophet held Fatima in his arms
and Gabriel revealed the following: Soon We will grant you something that
will make you happy (from Us). This was the second time this revelation
came; the first was in Mecca and it shows the importance of this event in
which he accepted this orphan into his family. What God meant was that
soon He would grant the thing to make him happy authorized by this
revelation, the right to intercede. Oh Muslims. Do not be disappointed. This
is the day for grabbing the commands of the Quran with a whole heart. The
Prophet took his uncle's orphan Fatima home. When he arrived home with
the orphan, his wife, the mother of the faithful, asked, "If God forgives half
of your *umma* because of this girl, will you be satisfied?" He said, "What are
you saying? I swear by God who has the soul of Muhammad in His hand
that even if one of my *umma* is left in hell, I will not be satisfied." Oh
disloyal *umma*! How you have forgotten fidelity to the faith! Why are you
abandoning the faith? Unfaithful *umma* why are you [women] cutting your
hair short and uncovering your heads? Oh unfaithful *umma*, why are you
unveiling yourself and going shamefully about the streets? Oh unfaithful
*umma*, why are you leaving the path of Lady Fatima, who will ask for
forgiveness for all the women of the *umma* [on judgment day]? Why are you
tearing her scarf? By doing this you displease her. We brothers, what can
we do? Uncovered Muslim women throw away the veil and walk in the
streets immodestly. Those women themselves will be cursed by God and they
will cause others to be cursed. Oh God! from the blessing of Fatima's face,
you forgive all our sins. May You give the women of Afghanistan their
required covering. By the blessing You gave Muhammad give us salvation
from our situation. ...

With this story of the little Fatima, the speaker has achieved the emotional
crescendo of his narration. Loud crying can be heard on the tape as the small girl
runs happily to give milk and dates to her father whom the audience knows is
already dead. Muhammad, who forsook vengeance on his uncle's behalf in the
previous section, upon deciding to adopt the child, receives confirmation of his
ability to intercede for the *umma*. In other words, Fatima's loss is the community's
gain. The value of sacrifice is clear. Furthermore, the Quran emphasizes the

protection of widows and orphans. Not only does the Prophet himself provide a concrete example of this caretaker role, he also provides this example in a context where it is particularly important, that is, in the situation of *jihad*, there are many widows and orphans for which the community at large must take reponsibility. The speaker juxtaposes this kind of exemplary responsibility with the contemporary symbol of the unveiled woman who lacks responsibility. As more Muslims take on self-interested motivations like the unveiled woman, the *umma* as a whole becomes corrupt.

## VII

**. . . A nation which sells its religion, sells its land and sells its honor. A nation without courage does not have the bravery to save its religion. In Islam honor has an important role. Muslims you should know this. A person without honor has no religion. God does not accept prayers and obedience from a person without courage. The religious obligations of a pimp will not be accepted [by God]. A pimp is a person who does not care about his family. If a man sees his wife with another man and does nothing, he is a whoremonger. This man's religious duties will not be accepted by God. . . . A person without courage has no religion. A person without religion has no homeland. . . .**

The speaker drives home the moral lesson of his oration by connecting Islam, honor, courage and territory. Ultimately the loss of these is attributed to the man who is a pimp. A man who fails to connect family, honor, and homeland to Islamic core values loses everything. This is what happened in Afghanistan. By implication in the new Islamic state that will be created after the *jihad*, religion, honor, courage, and territory will be restored.

## NOTES

1. For additional information and a different focus on the *jihad* cassette tapes, see "Women's Roles in the Afghanistan *Jihad*," *International Journal of Middle East Studies*, forthcoming.

2. Uhud and Badr were early important battles of the Muslims against the Meccans.

3. The word used here, *miraj*, refers to the highest point in the Prophet's life when he journeyed to heaven from Jerusalem on his winged horse.

4. Hind lost her father, son, brother, and uncle in the battles against the Muslims and swore not to sleep with her husband until they were avenged. After the conquest of Mecca, she was a convert to Islam. Her son Muawwiyya was the founder of the Umayyad dynasty.

5. Sunni Muslims recognize Abu Bakr as Muhammad's successor. He was known for always telling the truth.

# Chapter 10

## The Future

Why are the Ferghanachis important for the future of Afghanistan? As a fairly small-sized group within the larger ethnic communities of northern Afghanistan, does it make a difference that they continued to participate in the armed struggle and that some few remain in Pakistan among the refugee communities? The Ferghanachis provide a symbol of Russian/Soviet expansionism that serves as a constant reminder of how the Muslim lands of Central Asia have been transformed. Whether people consider the name they preferred in Afghanistan, *muhajir*, or the name most commonly used by other ethnic groups, Ferghanachi, the symbolic statement is as powerful. *Muhajir*, one who leaves the homeland when it has been taken by unbelievers, draws attention to the loss of the Central Asian khanates from the Islamic World and today, possibly, their triumphant return. Since the term resonates with events in the life of the Prophet, just as Muhammad triumphantly returned to Mecca, so too was this millenarian hope part of the everyday assumptions of the Ferghanachis. The hope of liberation of a homeland is powerful motivation and powerful prophecy.

Since all Afghans are now *muhajirs*, those who are *muhajirs* twice are even greater symbols of a seemingly inexorable historical process that many Afghans are determined to reverse. The resistance press and broadcasts in Pakistan have made many references to the fate of Bukhara. The existence of those who are visible reminders reinforces the determination that it should not happen again. Even if *muhajir* has become less a major part of identity, with so many who can claim this status, the term Ferghanachi, which uses the territorial label, still provides a geographical mnemonic for the interpretation of historical events and the corresponding hope for a better future.

Some western observers believed that Afghanistan might well be partitioned into north and south with the Soviet Union maintaining strong ties with the northern portion (Shroder 1989:112-116). In the days before the Soviet withdrawal, an actual Soviet annexation of the north was thought to be one possible settlement of the conflict. It is also likely that transportation, irrigation, and energy extraction development projects implemented by the Soviets in the north were part of their long-range integration policy. As Louis Dupree pointed out, this would have meant continued fighting, for the people there would certainly object to such an arrangement (1989:44). The battle for Kunduz in 1988 after the first phase of

151

the Soviet troop withdrawal indicates the importance the resistance placed on the region. The *mujahidin* were only forced to vacate Kunduz when it was bombed by the Soviet airforce, a violation of their negotiated withdrawal. It is the area farther to the west, especially Balkh and Jawzjan provinces, that was considered by western observers to be the key to Soviet plans and it is said that the resistance there was weak except in the more mountainous southern sections where the Hazaras were active (Newman 1988:729-739). Yet in Islamabad, Pakistan, during the winter of 1990, I met *mujahids* who were from Jawzjan province and who had recently returned from fighting there. It was the historical experience of people like the Ferghanachis which made the partition into a north and south Afghanistan an extremely unlikely outcome. Another solution much discussed in the western press is the return of Zahir Shah, the former king, who would form a new government based on the monarchy as a symbol of national unity. The problem is that Zahir Shah and indeed the Musahiban dynasty are not a symbol of national unity for groups like the Ferghanachis who, based on their historical experience, view the monarchy as pursuing a Pashtun chauvinist policy at the expense of national unity. The few gains made by minorities during the constitutional period were too little, too late. Furthermore, the use of what are perceived as Pashtun political institutions, for example, the *loya jirgah,* the Pashto word for tribal assembly, should at the very least be renamed and transformed so that they are no longer symbols of Pashtun dominance (Dupree 1989:46).

The northern minorities may be in an improved political position during the postwar period. More local autonomy in agriculture and mineral resources as a result of the war and resistance victories in the countryside may give groups leverage with any regime in Kabul. Unrest among Muslims in the Central Asian republics as a result of the Afghanistan War could mean that those from northern Afghanistan could also play a pivotal international role (Newell 1989:1100).

In recent years, the former Soviet Union has faced a crisis of increasing ethnic nationalism which in Central Asia appears to be inextricably mixed with a resurgence of Islamic observance. Muslims in the Central Asian republics are attending mosques, praying, fasting during the month of Ramadan, going on pilgrimages, circumcising young boys, incorporating Islam into marriage and death rituals, and even becoming involved in sufism (Rigby 1989:78, Bennigsen 1989). While the Afganistan War did not create this new ethnic/religious consciousness, it has provided new meaning and impetus for the revitalization movement. The Soviet withdrawal and the perceived weakness of their military machine at the hands of the Afghan resistance has allowed for new possibilities and hopes which play on the ethnic and religious identity of former Soviet Muslims. The Afghan resistance symbolizes both an Islamic and an ethnic consciousness since members of the resistance fighting in northern Afghanistan were co-ethnics with those on the other side of the border. The Afghan resistance made military advances across the Soviet border and also conducted an active campaign of smuggling cassette tapes on Islam into Soviet Central Asia, a fact mentioned in the Soviet Press (Bennigsen 1984; Canfield 1989:31). Distrust of Central Asians by ethnic Russian and other European groups within the Soviet Union also was exacerbated by the Afghanistan War. Initially, the Soviet invasion force had many Central Asian troops since the intervention was conducted by the Turkestan Military District (Jukes 1989:87). There were continuing rumors of unreliability fostered when these troops were withdrawn in 1980. In fact, many of the Uzbek soldiers were reservists who went home when their 90 day tour of duty was over. But Russians apparently resented the fact that these troops were spared while Russian boys were killed in what was essentially a "Central Asian dispute" (Jukes: 1989:88). The Afghanistan War thus mutually distanced Europeans and Asian peoples of the former Soviet Union from each other.

As the Central Asian republics begin to develop an independent course, the Ferghanachis are renewing their ties to their original homeland. For some, the historical process has come full circle. There are those who, finding the situation in Afghanistan too unsettled, moved from Kunduz back across the border into Tajikistan in 1992. Others in Saudi Arabia and the United States are exploring new financial and resettlement opportunities in Uzbekistan which has recognized the transnationals as full citizens. Because of the unrest in Tajikistan, there are reports that some there have moved across the border into northern Afghanistan once again, thereby enacting another version of the original migration.

# Epilogue

## The Ferghanachis in the United States

During the 1980s, only a few thousand Afghans were allowed to emigrate to the United States each year (Refugee Reports 1991:16). Most of these Afghans were Pashtuns, often of an urban background. Some small numbers of Ferghanachis have come to the United States; the largest communities are in the Washington D.C. and New York metropolitan areas. Here they joined other Uzbeks including some Ferghanachis who had come to the United States from Afghanistan and Soviet Central Asia before the Afghanistan War. The Ferghanachis often seek to own small businesses in the United States, a continuation of their merchant status.

There are many rapid changes that confront the new arrivals. English replaces Dari, Afghan Persian, as the language used with outsiders. Thus Uzbek, the in-group language, is retained and Dari tends to disappear, especially among younger speakers. This fact distances individuals from Afghanistan and makes it more likely that the young will not return. Children who come to the United States before adolescence speak English with no trace of an accent within a few years. Their language is replete with references to popular music, video games, and other elements of American popular culture. Often they come to prefer fast foods like french fries and pizza to the traditional *pilaw* of Afghanistan.

One obvious change in the lifestyle of the Ferghanachis is the abandonment of veiling and modest dress for women. Except on Islamic holidays and the rare woman who adopts Saudi-style modest dress with only face and hands revealed, most women quickly choose western-type clothing including slacks and short sleeves. Older women may retain flowing dresses and headscarves but on the whole dress is Americanized. Men wear western-style clothes for work, a pattern which was already used for certain occupations in Afghanistan although they occasionally wear traditional clothes for lounging around the house or sleeping.

The change in dress also symbolizes a change in male/female interaction. In the United States, behavior formerly associated with only the closest relatives is expanded to encompass those who are not related but are in the ethnic group. At parties, and dinners during the fast month of Ramadan, or wedding celebrations, for example, there is less separation of the sexes. Usually, people sit down together as if they were from the same household. Men and women may sit in different sections of the same room or in adjoining rooms. Women and men even dance traditional dances in front of everyone including the opposite sex. In many respects, the pattern resembles that found in Uzbekistan as depicted in Soviet media. In a few households, a stricter separation is maintained for special dinners but even in these cases there is more cross greeting and interaction than before.

Little socializing is done with people outside the ethnic group. In the cases with which I am most familiar, teenage dating is still not permitted.

Other changes are the increased use of cigarettes and alcohol at parties by both men and women. This use of liquor, a pattern already occurring among certain classes in Kabul, has meant that behavioral judgments no longer link Islam and ethnicity. For example, a woman in Kunduz once said, "Uzbek men don't drink. They are good Muslims." The woman can no longer make such a statement and it really was not accurate even in the 1970s.

Periodically, some of the men of the community talk about buying a plot of land and developing it themselves so that they can live more Islamically as a community. They face the hurdles of the disparate wishes and interests that their wives and children have developed in addition to the financial burden of buying the land and building houses. The Ferghanachis are dispersed through the metropolitan areas and do not have their own mosques. The best some can do is to send their children to religious school once a week or teach them at home when they can. It is the telephone and the automobile which now connect the community.

As time goes on, the Ferghanachis increasingly take on the typical character-istics of an ethnic group in the United States. Certain symbols, often foods or celebrations, reinforce ethnicity but daily routine continues through the life of nuclear families who go their own way. At parties, traditional foods such as the various kinds of rice dishes and occasionally noodles such as *mantu* reinforce the feelings of community, but in the home, the children eat fast food in front of the television set or they eat at the mall. A family has *pilaw* most nights but who teaches girls to cook in the traditional way? At weddings, everyone sings the Uzbek wedding song, "*Yar Yar*," but the wedding is at a rented hall or hotel with both men and women present, dancing together western-style. Some parts of traditional ways are retained and given great symbolic importance, while other parts are lost.

While not common yet, most informants could name individuals who had married non-Muslims. In fact, a major crisis occurred when a girl eloped with a young Christian man. According to Islam, a Muslim man can marry one of the people of the book, that is, a woman who is Jewish or Christian but a Muslim woman must marry a Muslim. Furthermore, the group that takes a wife is generally considered superior to the group who gives one who lose her labor, her children, and the bridewealth (Tapper 1991). The elopement was thus dishonorable in the extreme. The girl refused to return home; the shame of the event was so great that people who did not even know the family cried. The young man was persuaded to recite the *shahada*, the profession of faith, but everyone knew that it was hypocritical. The situation was so bad that some seriously began to reconsider their stay in the United States. Though many had become U.S. citizens, people began to talk of moving to Saudi Arabia, returning to Pakistan or of going to live in Uzbekistan "where at least the people are Muslims." With the strong Ferghanachi community in Saudi Arabia and intermarriage with Saudi citizens, much movement between Saudi Arabia and the United States takes place. Individuals thus become bicultural or even tricultural and they become adept at switching their behavior and their language appropriately. Saudi Arabia may prove to be one lasting homeland but the Ferghanachis there are likely to assimilate to Arab culture.

It has now been sixty years since parents or grandparents left the Central Asian homeland. Through sojourns in Afghanistan, Pakistan, and other parts of the east and west, the Ferghanachis have so far survived. Their story is in many ways quintessential for the twentieth century--the loss of home and the never-ending search to find one.

# Glossary

This glossary includes words of general importance most of which are also defined in the text itself. Other words of less significance are clearly defined in the text and are not included here.

*adat*-customary law

*almasti* (*albasti*)-an impure witchlike creature who has special powers

*amir*-prince, lord, or nobleman; the title of the ruler of the nineteenth century state of Bukhara

*buzkashi*-a sport played on horseback in which an animal carcass is carried to a goal

*chadari*-the Afghan veil; a full enveloping pleated garment with mesh over the face

*chapan*-the cotton, or cotton/silk cloak worn by men of northern Afghanistan and Central Asia

*ghazi*-one who kills an unbeliever during jihad

*giraw*-a form of lending arrangement in which the lender of capital receives the use of property for some years. If the loan is not repaid, the lender keeps the property.

*hadith*-codes of conduct based on the Prophet's words and deeds

*hijab*-modest dress for women

*hijrat*-migration for the sake of Islam

*Islam*-submission to God

*jihad*-spiritual struggle, usually translated as holy war

*kocha*-a lane or street connecting several households

*madrassah*-advanced school of Islamic learning

*mahalla*-a neighborhood often founded by a particular ethnic group

*maktab*-primary school

*mawlewi*-religious scholar

*muhajir*-one who migrates for the sake of Islam; emigrant; refugee

*mujahid*-one engaged in struggle for the sake of Islam; one who is in the holy war

*mullah*-one who has some Islamic religious education; a learned man

*Muslim*-one who submits to God

*musafir*-a traveller; one on a journey or passing through

*pilaw*-rice casserole; typical main dish at a meal

*qari*-one who has memorized the Quran; religious authority

*qawm*-ethnic group; tribe

*qazi*-judge

*qiyamat*-the time of final judgment by God

*Quran*-Islam's holy book; Muhammad's revelations from God

*samanak* (*sumulak*-Uzbek)-a cooked pudding made from the juice of ground, newly sprouted wheat distributed around the New Year, March 21.

*sayid*-one who claims descent from the Prophet; often a title

*shahid*-martyr; a witness for Islam to the death

*shariat*-the righteous path; Islamic law based on the Quran and hadith; canon law

*ulema*-Islamic scholars and clergy

*umma*-worldwide Muslim community whose origins were in Medina at Muhammad's time

*waqf*- land given over as a trust whose endowment is used to support Islamic institutions such as mosques and madrassahs

*watan*-homeland; country

*zakat*-alms, the giving of which is one of the five responsibilities of all Muslims

# References

Akramov, Z. M.
    1960    *Zhemchuzhina Srednei Azii*. Moscow: Gosudarstvennoe
        Izdatel'stvo Geograficheskoi Literatury.

Alderson, A. D. and Iz, Fahir
    1959    *The Concise Oxford Turkish Dictionary*. Oxford: The Clarendon
        Press.

Andreev, M.S.
    1928    Poiezdka letom g. 1928 v Kansanskii Raion (sever Fergany). *The
        Society for Studies of Tajikistan and Iranian Peoples beyond its
        Boundaries* I: 109-130.

Arberry, A. J.
    1976    The Koran Interpreted. 7th printing. New York: Macmillan.

Aziz, Sultan
    1987    Leadership Dilemmas: Challenges and Responses. *Afghan
        Resistance: The Politics of Survival*. (Grant Farr and John
        Merriam, eds.), pp.51-70. Boulder: Westview Press.

Bacon, Elizabeth
    1966    *Central Asians under Russian Rule*. Ithaca: Cornell U. Press.

Barfield, T. J.
    1981    *The Central Asian Arabs: Pastoral Nomadism in Transition*.
        Austin: University of Texas Press.

Barth. Fredrik
    1965    *Political Leadership among Swat Pathans*. revised ed. New York:
        Humanities Press.

    1969    *Ethnic Groups and Boundaries*. Boston: Little, Brown and Co.

Barthold, W.W.
    1934    "Sart," in *Encyclopedia of Islam*. (M. Th. Houtsma, A. J.
        Wensinck, H. A. R. Gibb, W. Heffening, E. Levi-Provencal, eds.),
        pp. 175-176. Leyden: E. J. Brill Ltd.

Becker, Seymour
    1968    *Russia's Protectorates in Central Asia: Bukhara and Khiva.*
            Cambridge, Mass: Harvard U. Press.

Bennigsen, Alexandre
    1984    Mullahs, Mujahidin, and Soviet Muslims. *Problems of Communism.*
            Nov.-Dec.:28-44.

    1989    Islam in Retrospect. *Central Asian Survey* 8(1):89-109.

Bennigsen, Alexandre and Lemercier-Quelquejay, Chantal
    1967    *Islam in the Soviet Union.* New York: Praeger.

Beveridge, Annette (Trans.)
    1912    *Babur-nama, the Memoirs of Babur.* London: Luzac and Co.

Boesen, Inger
    1988    What Happens to Honour in Exile? Continuity and Change among
            Afghan Refugees in *The Tragedy of Afghanistan.* (Bo Huldt and
            Erland Jansson, eds.), pp. 219-239. London: Croom Helm.

Byron, Robert
    1937    *The Road to Oxiana.* London: Jonathan Cape Ltd.

Canfield, Robert L.
    1973    *Faction and Conversion in a Plural Society: Religious Alignments
            in the Hindu Kush.* Ann Arbor: The University of Michigan Press.

    1985    Islamic Sources of Resistance. *Orbis.* (spring),   pp.57-71.

    1986    Ethnic, Regional and Sectarian Alignments in Afghanistan. *The
            State, Religion, and Ethnic Politics: Afghanistan, Iran, and
            Pakistan.* (Ali Banuazizi and  Myron Weiner, eds.), pp.75-103.
            Syracuse: Syracuse University Press.

    1989    The Collision of Evolutionary Process and Islamic Ideology in
            Greater Central Asia. *Afghanistan and the Soviet Union: Collision
            and Transformation.* (Milan Hauner and Robert Canfield, eds.),
            pp.13-39. Boulder: Westview Press.

1991    *Turko-Persia in Historical Perspective.* Cambridge: Cambridge
        University Press.

Caroe, Olaf
    1967    *Soviet Empire: the Turks of Central Asia and Stalinism.* 2nd ed.
            New York: St. Martin's Press.

Carrere d'Encausse, Helene
    1967    Organizing and Colonizing the Conquered Territories, in *Central
            Asia, a Century of Russian Rule*, ed. E. Allworth. New York:
            Columbia U. Press, 151-71.

    1988    *Islam and the Russian Empire.* Berkeley: University of California
            Press.

Casson, Ronald
    1974    Semantic Structure and Social Structure in a Central Anatolian
            Village. *Anthropological Quarterly* 47(4):347-373.

Central Asian Research Centre
    1959    The Basmachi Movement. *Central Asian Review* 7(3):236-
            250.

Chagatay, Babur and Sjoberg, A.N.
    1955    Notes on the Uzbek Culture of Central Asia. *Texas Journal of
            Science* 7(1):72-112.

Chaliand, Gerard
    1982    *Report from Afghanistan.* New York: Viking Press.

Dupree, Louis
    1989    Post-Withdrawal Afghanistan: Light at the End of the Tunnel.
            *Soviet Withdrawal from Afghanistan.* (Amin Saikal and William
            Maley, eds.), pp. 29-51. Cambridge: Cambridge University Press.

Dupree, Nancy
    1967    *The Road to Balkh.* Kabul: The Afghan Tourist Organization.

Edwards, David
    1987    Origins of the Anti-Soviet Jihad. *Afghan Resistance: The Politics
            of Survival.* (Grant Farr and John Merriam, eds.), pp.21-80.
            Boulder: Westview Press.

Eisenstadt, S. N.
    1974    Preface, in *The Predicament of Homecoming,* Shlomo Deshen and
            Moshe Skokeid [authors]. Ithaca: Cornell University Press.

Fallers, Lloyd and Margaret Fallers,
    1976    Sex Roles in Edremit, in *Mediterranean Family Structures.* (J. G.
            Peristiany, ed.), pp.243-260. Cambridge: Cambridge University
            Press.

Farr, Grant
    1987    The New Afghan Middle Class as Refugees and Insurgents. *Afghan
            Resistance: The Politics of Survival.* (Grant Farr and John
            Merriam, eds.), pp.127-150. Boulder: Westview Press.

Gall, Sandy
    1988    *Afghanistan: Agony of a Nation.* London: The Bodley Head.

Gault, Paul
    1892    Position Ethnologique des Peuples du Ferganah. *L'Anthropologie*
            3:55-65.

Good, Mary Jo
    1977    Of Blood and Babies: The Relationship of Popular Islamic
            Physiology to Fertility. Paper presented to a colloquium: Biology,
            Society, and History in Islam, Department of History and Middle
            East Center, University of Pennsylvania.

Haim, S.
    1973    *The One Volume Persian-English Dictionary.* Teheran: Librairie-
            Imprimerie Beroukhim.

Jarring, Gunnar
    1937a   The New Afghanistan, in *Svenska Orientsallskapets Arsbok.*
            Stockholm: Bokforlags Aktiebologet Thule, pp. 131-145.

1937b    The Uzbek Dialect of Qilich. *Lund Universitets Arsskrift* 33, I:23-45.

1938     Uzbek Texts from Afghan Turkestan. *Lund Universitets Arsskrift* 34, I:1-246

1939     The Classification of Turk Tribes in Afghanistan. *Lund Universitets Arsskrift* 35, IV:3-104.

Jukes, Geoffrey
1989     The Soviet Armed Forces and the Afghan War. *The Soviet Withdrawal from Afghanistan*. (Amin Saikal and William Maley, eds.), pp. 82-100. Cambridge: Cambridge University Press.

Khuri, Fuad
1976     The Effects of Family Ties on Capital Formation and Investment, Economic Aid and Household Organization in Two Suburbs of Beirut, in *Kinship and Modernization in Mediterranean Society.* (J. G. Peristiany, ed.), pp. 13-29. Rome: The Center for Mediterranean Studies.

Klass, Rosanne
1985     The New Holocaust. *National Review.* Oct. 4, pp. 28-29.

Krader, Lawrence
1963     *Social Organization of the Mongol-Turkic Pastoral Nomads.* Bloomington: University of Indiana Press.

Kushkeki, Burkhaduddin Khan-i
1926     Kattagan and Badakhshan. *The Society of Studies of Tajikistan and Iranian Peoples beyond its Boundaries* II:1-248.

Laber, Jeri and Barnett Rubin
1988     *A Nation is Dying.* Evanston: Northwestern University Press.

Lemercier-Quelquejay, Chantal and Alexandre Bennigsen
1984     Soviet Experience of Muslim Guerilla Warfare and the War in Afghanistan. *The USSR and the Muslim World.* (Yaacov Roi, ed.), pp.206-214. London: George Allen and Unwin.

Lorimer, Frank
    1946    *The Population of the Soviet Union: History and Prospects.*
        Geneva: League of Nations.

Malkki, Liisa
    1992    National Geographic: The Rooting of Peoples and the
        Territorialization of National Identity among Scholars and
        Refugees. *Cultural Anthropology* 7(1):24-44.

Meakin, Annette
    1908    Turkestan, in *Women of all Nations*, Vol. 4. (T.A. Joyce, ed.), 646-
        653. London: Cassell and Co., Ltd.

Michel, Aloys A.
    1959    *The Kabul, Kunduz, and Helmand Valleys and the National*
        *Economy of Afghanistan.* Foreign Field Research Program, Office
        of Naval Research, Report No. 5. Washington D.C.: National
        Academy of Sciences--National Research Council, Division of
        Earth Sciences.

Mills, Margaret
    1991    *Rhetorics and Politics in Afghan Traditional Storytelling.*
        Philadelphia: University of Pennsylvania Press.

Naby, Eden
    1984    The Uzbeks in Afghanistan. *Central Asian Survey* 3(1):1-21.

    1986a    The Changing Role of Islam as a Unifying Force in Afghanistan.
        *The State, Religion, and Ethnic Politics: Afghanistan, Iran, and*
        *Pakistan.* (Ali Banuazizi and Myron Weiner, eds.), pp. 124-154.
        Syracuse: Syracuse University Press.

    1986b    The Concept of Jihad in Opposition to Communist Rule: Turkestan
        and Afghanistan. *Studies in Comparative Communism* XIX
        (3/4):287-300.

    1988a    Ethnic Factors in Afghanistan's Future. *The Tragedy of*
        *Afghanistan.* (Bo Huldt and Erland Jansson, eds.), pp. 62-74. New
        York: Croom Helm.

1988b    Islam within the Afghan Resistance. *Third World Quarterly*
         10(2):787-805.

Newell, Richard
    1989    Post-Soviet Afghanistan: The Position of the Minorities. *Asian
            Survey* XXIX (11):1090-1111.

Newman, Joseph
    1988    The Future of Northern Afghanistan. *Asian Survey* XXVIII
            (7):729-739.

Oshanin. L. V.
    1964    *Anthropological Composition of the Population of Central Asia
            and the Ethnogenesis of its People.* Cambridge, Mass.: The
            Peabody Museum.

Park, Alexander
    1957    *Bolshevism in Turkestan 1917-1927.* New York:
            Columbia University Press.

Pipes, Richard
    1964    *The Formation of the Soviet Union, Communism and Nationalism.*
            revised ed. Cambridge, Mass.: Harvard University Press.

Raun, Alo
    1969    Basic Course in Uzbek. *Indiana University Publications, Uralic
            and Altaic Series* 59: 1-271.

Refugee Reports
    1991    Afghan Refugees Admitted to the United States. Washington D.C.:
            U.S. Committee for Refugees XII(2):16.

Rigby, T. H.
    1989    The Afghan Conflict and Soviet Domestic Politics. *The Soviet
            Withdrawal from Afghanistan.* (Amin Saikal and William Maley,
            eds.), pp. 67-81. Cambridge: Cambridge University Press.

Rosaldo, Renato
    1989    Culture and Truth: The Remaking of Social Analysis. Boston:
            Beacon Press.

Roy, Olivier
1985 *L'Afghanistan: Islam et Modernity Politique*. Paris: Editions du Seuil.

Rywkin, Michael
1963 *Russia in Central Asia*. New York: Collier Books.

1984 National Symbiosis: Vitality, Religion, Identity, Allegiance. *The USSR and the Muslim World*. (Yaacov Roi, ed.), pp. 3-15. London: George Allen and Unwin.

Said, Edward
1979 Zionism from the Standpoint of its Victims. Social Text 1:7-58.

Schuyler, Eugene
1877 *Turkistan: Notes of a Journey in Russian Turkistan, Khokand, Bukhara, and Kuldja*. Vols, I and II. New York: Scribner, Armstrong and Co.

Shahrani, M. Nazif
1986 State Building and Social Fragmentation in Afghanistan: A Historical Perspective. *State, Religion, and Ethnic Politics: Afghanistan, Iran, and Pakistan*. (Ali Banuazizi and Myron Weiner, eds.), pp. 23-74. Syracuse: Syracuse University Press.

1991 Local Knowledge of Islam and Social Discourse in Afghanistan and Turkistan in the Modern Period. *Turko-Persia in Historical Perspective*. (Robert Canfield, ed.), Cambridge: Cambridge University Press.

Shahrani, M. Nazif and Robert Canfield (eds.)
1984 *Revolutions and Rebellions in Afghanistan*. Berkeley: University of California Institute of International Studies.

Shalinsky, Audrey
1979 History as Self-Image: The Case of Central Asian Emigres in Afghanistan. *Journal of South Asian and Middle Eastern Studies* 3(2):7-19.

1980    Group Prestige in Northern Afghanistan: The Case of an Interethnic Wedding. *Ethnic Groups* 2:269-282.

1982-83 Islam and Ethnicity: The Northern Afghanistan Perspective. *Central Asian Survey* 1(2):71-85.

1984a   Ethnic Reactions to the Current Regime in Afghanistan: A Case Study. *Central Asian Survey* 3(4):49-60.

1984b   The Battle for the Bride: The Wedding as Rite of Passage in Northern Afghanistan. *The Eastern Anthropologist* 37(1):1-13.

1986a   Reason, Desire and Sexuality: The Meaning of Gender in Northern Afghanistan. *Ethos* 14(4):223-243.

1986b   Uzbek Ethnicity in Northern Afghanistan. Die *Ethnischen Gruppen Afghanistans.* (E. Orywal, ed.), Universität zu Köln, Institut für Völkerkunde. General Editor, Tübinger Atlas des Vörderen Orients, TAVO. Publisher: L. Reichert Verlag, Weisbaden.

1989a   Talking About Marriage: Fate and Choice in the Social Discourse of Traditional Northern Afghanistan. *Anthropos* 84:133-140.

1989b   Women's Relationships in Traditional Northern Afghanistan. *Central Asian Survey* 8(1):117-129.

1990    The Significance of Islam in Pre-1978 Northern Afghanistan: An Urban Uzbek Case. *Central Asian Survey* (Society for Central Asian Studies) 9(4):99-108.

Shaniiazov, K.
1974    On the Traditional Uzbek Cuisine. *Soviet Anthropology and Archeology* 12(4):32-58.

Shroder, John
1989    Afghanistan Resources and Soviet Policy in Central and South Asia. *Afghanistan and the Soviet Union: Collision and Transformation.* (Milan Haunder and Robert Canfield, eds.), pp. 101-119. Boulder: Westview Press.

Slobin, Mark
    1976    *Music in the Culture of Northern Afghanistan.* Tuscon: The
            University of Arizona Press.

Smith, H. H., Bernier, D., Bunge, F., Rintz, F. C., Shinn, R. S., and Teleki, S.
    1973    *Area Handbook for Afghanistan.* 4th ed. Washington D.C.: U.S.
            Government Printing Office.

Snesarev, G. P.
    1970-74 Remnants of Pre-Islamic Beliefs and Rituals among the Khorezm
            Uzbeks. *Soviet Anthropology and Archeology.* excerpts. Part 1,
            Vol. 9(3): 204-225; Part 2, Vol.9(4): 329-352; Part 3, Vol.10(1):3-
            36; Part 4, Vol. 10(3):253-289; Part 5, Vol. 11(3):219-236; Part 6,
            Vol. 11(4):33-80; Part 7, Vol. 12(4):3-31; Part 8, Vol. 13(1):3-37;
            Part 9, Vol. 13(2):3-32.

Spencer, Robert
    1960    Aspects of Turkish Kinship and Social Structure. *Anthropological
            Quarterly* 33: 40-50.

*Statistical Pocket-book of Afghanistan*
    1972    Kabul: Ministry of Planning.

Tapper, Nancy
    1983    Abd al-Rahman's Northwest Frontier: The Pashtun Colonization of
            Afghan Turkistan. *The Conflict of Tribe and State in Iran and
            Afghanistan.* (Richard Tapper, ed.), pp.233-261. New York: St.
            Martin's Press.

    1991    *Bartered Brides: Politics, Gender and Marriage in an Afghan
            Tribal Society.* Cambridge: Cambridge University Press.

Wheeler, Geoffrey
    1964    *The Modern History of Soviet Central Asia.* London: Weindenfeld
            and Nicholson.

Wood, John
    1872    *A Journey to the Source of the River Oxus.* 2nd ed. London: John
            Murray.

Zhilina, A. N.
   1974      Traditional Features in the Modern Khorezmian Dwelling. *Soviet Anthropology and Archeology*   12(4):59-81

# Index

## A

Abbassids of Baghdad, 7
Abdul Aziz
    cotton production by, 27
Abortion, attitudes toward, 79
Abu Bakr, 149
'Adili, Mawlewi Abdul Fattah
    in memory of, 118
    military activities of, 119
Afghan nation-state, development of, 110
Afghan native,
    distinguished from non-native, 97
Afghan resistance, 152
Afghan-American Educational
    Commission, 2, 39
Afghanistan
    possible partitioning of, 151
    return to, 126
Afghanistan Studies Center at the University of Nebraska, Omaha, 127
Afghanistan War, 153
Age
    as basis of respect, 86
    determining child's, 66
    role of in determining community
        leadership, 86
Air travel, Kunduz to Kabul, 29
Ajash, Abdullah
    in battle of Uhud, 144
Alcoholic beverages
    conflicts over use of, 91
    drinking before marriage ritual, 75
    increasing use of in U.S., 156
Alms
    given to poor, 93
    payment of prohibited, 22
Amin, Hafizullah
    seizes power, 112
Amir of Bukhara, 15
    flees, 19
    signs treaty, 17
Amu Darya River, 7, 29
    from other side of, 97
Andijan, 2
    1898 revolt in, 18
Andreev, Mikhail, 12
    report by, 49
Angel Gabriel, 145

## B

Angel group, 126
Animal bazaar, 41, (photograph), 34
Animal
    care of, (photograph), 43
    classification of, 66
Ataturk, Kemal, 19
Babur
    defeat of, 8
    loss of empire by, 15
Bakr, Siddiq Abu, 147
Balkh
    as capital of Turkestan, 15
Basmachi revolt, 20
Basmachis
    as national liberation movement, 19
    defined, 19
    victories against Bolsheviks of, 20
Battle for Kunduz (1988), 151
Battle of Uhud, 140, 142, 143, 144, 145
Bazaar
    as male focal point, 85
    Kunduz, 32, 101
    women visiting the, 80
Beirut
    three-generation households in, 57
Bilaterality, 64
Birth
    social impact on woman of a, 65
Bonds, household, 59
Book of Martyrs, 118
Bread
    as staple diet, 30
    serving of, 51
Bribery
    in elections, 84
    of Khalq official, 112
    of police, 63
Bride
    belongings of, 47
    control over by other women, 70
    gifts given to the, 72
    strict seclusion of, 73
    welcoming rituals, 73
Bride-welcoming, 73
    ceremony in Karachi, 133
Bridegifts, 131
Brideprice
    setting of the, 69
Bughra Khan, 13
Bukhara, emirate of, 13

173